Loved for who I am

Loved for who I am

Carlo Maria Martini

A Redemptorist Publication

Published by
Redemptorist Publications
A Registered Charity Limited by guarantee. Registered in England 3261721

Copyright © 2000 Redemptorist Publications

Original text: "Tu mi scruti e mi conosci" by Carlo Maria Martini published in 1999
by Ancora Editrice Milan Italy
Translation: First Edition Translations Cambridge England

Editor: Fr Ed Hone C.Ss.R.

Design: Rosemarie Pink

Cover picture: Photonica

ISBN 0 85231 216 4

This edition printed September 2000

Printed by Estudios Gráficos Zure, Spain

Redemptorist
P U B L I C A T I O N S
Alphonsus House Chawton Hampshire GU34 3HQ
Telephone 01420 88222   Fax 01420 88805
rp@redempt.org   www.redempt.org

Contents

Contents continued

Loved for who I am

Preface

'Loved for who I am' is adapted from a Lenten retreat given by Cardinal Martini, Archbishop of Milan to students of the school of the Seveso Diocesan Seminary. It examines two questions: "Who am I?" and "Who, Lord, are you?"

The Archbishop, as always, allows himself to be led by the word of God through the *lectio divina* or *holy reading* of various passages from the Old and New Testaments, bringing to life all the strength and energy of the word of God.

Lectio Divina

Lectio Divina is the prayerful reading of Scripture. Contemplating the sacred texts helps us understand their deeper meaning. In Lectio Divina, we read, we reflect and we pray.

Loved for who I am is divided into nine dialogues. Each dialogue will prove helpful not only for young people, but also for teachers and all who are in some way responsible for guiding young people. The quotations from the Bible are so organised as to make the retreat a model of how best to make the word of God accessible to the mind and heart of the young and the not-so-young.

This brings to mind the gospel saying quoted by Pope John Paul ll in his letter to the young people of the world: "Jesus looked steadily at him and he was filled with love for him" (Mark 10:21). This is the beginning of all true communication. To gather young people together, to understand and listen, to help them and feel an affinity with them when they open their hearts, to be able to see what motivates them, it is necessary to see them clearly and lovingly through the eyes of Jesus.

Introduction

We begin with a prayer.

> "We stand before you, Lord, not knowing how to talk to you, and so we rely on the words with which you have inspired your prophets: 'Yahweh, you examine me and know me, …you understand my thoughts from afar. You…know every detail of my conduct.' (See psalm 139.)

> You know the journey which we are about to make during these days together. You know what we want and what we ought to say to you. Grant that we may find the right words. Your wisdom is overwhelming and we shall try to comprehend it, to understand that you know us, you love us and that we are known to you. Mary, Mother of Jesus, you who know us, because we are your children, be with us now and pray for us."

> *Yahweh is the name used extensively in the New Jerusalem Bible to signify The Lord, or God. Yahweh (YHWH, Jehovah) is related to the Hebrew verb 'to be'. So the Lord is the one who 'is'.*

The Theme of the retreat

I had spent a long time trying to decide on a theme for these spiritual exercises when I remembered the *Message* which Pope John Paul II addressed to young people for the World Day of Peace some years ago. It notes two basic questions which are linked to one another; and the whole direction of our lives depends upon our answer to them.

Pope John Paul says:

"Among the inevitable questions that you must ask yourselves, the first and foremost is this: What is your idea of man? What, to you, makes up the dignity and the greatness of a human being? This is a question that you young people have to ask yourselves but which you also put to the generation that has preceded you, to your parents and to all those who at various levels have had the responsibility of caring for the goods and values of the world."

After explaining how important it is that society helps young people answer this question, and highlighting the serious responsibility borne by those who direct young people towards the wrong answers, the Pope concludes:

> *"Ask yourselves what kind of people you want yourselves and your fellow human beings to be, what kind of culture you want to build"*

"Ask yourselves what kind of people you want yourselves and your fellow human beings to be, what kind of culture you want to build. Ask yourselves these questions and do not be afraid of the answers, even if they will require of you a change of direction in your thoughts and loyalties."

Who am I?

We can make the question *What is your idea of man?* even simpler by expressing it as *Who am I?* This may seem superfluous, but it is in fact anything but. If we think carefully about it, this is what we ask ourselves every morning when we wake up and look around us: *Where am I? Who am I? What am I doing?*

Pope John XXIII used to tell people that he was sometimes kept awake at night worrying about the seriousness of the problems he had to face, and he used to find himself saying: "Oh well, tomorrow we'll ask the Pope." Immediately afterwards, however, it would occur to him: "But I am the Pope!" He realised that he himself had to respond to a series of complex situations, that he was the one who had been called on to bear great responsibilities.

Who am I? is therefore a very challenging question, because it prompts each one of us to understand ourselves as a person, our personality, our mission, our calling, and our responsibility in the context of today's world. The mass media (and especially large advertising companies) project an image at young men and women which puts on them an identity which matches high profile examples. *Who am I?* I am someone who has to put on that suit, who must wear that cap, play that sport, consume a certain drink.

Totalitarian governments and ideologies expend great energy to ensure that people, especially young people, conform to their way of thinking, or believe in and work for certain approved social and political ends. The question: *Who am I?* is therefore vitally important. Answering it is, to a certain extent, becoming aware of your own personality, of your own calling. Failing to answer means we allow others to answer for us, to manipulate us for their own ends. Each one of us needs to be able to find our answer truthfully from within ourselves.

Who is my God?

But, Pope John Paul goes on to say, the first question leads "to another even more basic and fundamental question: *Who is your God?*"

> *The theme which I wish to explore with you amounts to an in-depth examination of the two questions posed by the Pope: Who am I? and Who are You?"*

"We cannot define our notion of man without defining an absolute, a fullness of truth, of beauty and of goodness by which we allow our lives to be guided. Thus it is true that a human being, 'the visible image of an invisible God,' cannot answer the question about who he or she is without at the same time declaring who his or her God is. It is impossible to restrict this question to the sphere of people's private existence. It is impossible to separate this question from the history of nations…Everyone knows, albeit obscurely and with dread, that wherever God dies in the conscience of the human person, there follows inevitably the death of man, the image of God."

The theme which I wish to explore with you amounts to an in-depth examination of the two questions posed by the Pope: *Who am I?* and *Who are You?"*

Method for private meditation

In order to answer these questions, we will select some extracts from the Gospels and from the Old Testament. We will begin with a short reading, following the method of the *lectio divina*; this will be followed by meditation in order to understand the messages of the biblical text. You should then continue on your own with reflection and prayer.

How should you meditate on your own? I suggest five methods which you can use for half an hour or more. You needn't go through them all, one after the other: you may choose to focus on just one method.

1. *Re-read and underline*. Go back to the passage in the Bible and re-read it, underlining those words you think are important; put an exclamation mark or a question mark where appropriate.

2. *Look for Biblical parallels*. Try to think whether there are similar passages to the ones you are studying elsewhere in the Bible. These parallels can be of two types: a *story* in which the same events are narrated (I will give you a few examples) or a *prayer*. You should look for a prayer which is relevant to the passage. This is why I have given you the Book of Psalms! There are verses or entire psalms which provide a commentary in prayer to the page we are reading. The first six verses of Psalm 139, which we began by reviewing, are a commentary, for example, on the questions *Who am I* and *Who are You?* The psalmist actually says: Yahweh, you examine me and know me.

3. *Ask*. Ask the Lord something: "Lord, what shall I ask you about this passage, this reflection? What do I need? Lord, what do I want you to help me understand?" Know that when you are asking, you are already praying.

> 4. *Offer yourself.* Do not merely ask, give as well: "Lord, I want to offer you something, I want to make you a gift of some part of my life. What do you want of me? What do you want me to give you?"
>
> 5. *Plan.* Drawing on the passage, I can understand that it is important to accomplish something, perhaps to carry out a duty more conscientiously than I have done up till now, or to undertake something new.

If you try to cover all these five points, you need more than half an hour to complete them. However long you spend, you will have worked towards achieving personal insight into the passage.

A suggestion

I believe it would be useful for you to ask yourself:
  – What do I expect from this retreat?
  – What would I like?
  – What do I want?
This is a single question, even though it may have many forms, and it is very important because it determines how your energies are mobilised. For this reason I suggest that you devote some time to reflection so that you will be able to answer seriously and sincerely. It may help you to say Psalm 139 slowly, as a prayer.

A Prayer to begin with

"Lord, you have guided me here and have led me to this time. Now I need to know who I am and who You are. And, before I begin, I need to know what I expect and what I want. Rid me of all meaningless words and grant that I may arrive at the heart of things.

You see my deepest desires, my readiness to accept your Word. You know my hopes: grant me clear-sightedness, that I may see myself, and reveal yourself to me in the power of your Gospel."

A Quotation

From Pope John Paul II's Message to mark the World Day of Peace, 1st January 1985; paragraphs 3, 4 & 5.

"Young people, do not be afraid of your own youth
The first appeal I want to address to you, young men and women of today, is this: Do not be afraid! Do not be afraid of your own youth, and of those deep desires you have for happiness, for truth, for beauty and for lasting love!

Sometimes people say that society is afraid of these powerful desires of young people, and that you yourselves are afraid of them. Do not be afraid! When I look at you, the young people, I feel great gratitude and hope. The future far into the next century lies in your hands. The future of peace lies in your hearts. To construct history, as you can and must, you must free history from the false paths it is pursuing. To do this, you must be people with a deep trust in man and a deep trust in the grandeur of the human vocation – a vocation to be pursued with respect for truth and for the dignity and inviolable rights of the human person.

What I see arising in you is a new awareness of your responsibility and a fresh sensitivity to the needs of your fellow human beings. You are touched by the hunger for peace that so many share with you. You are troubled by so much injustice around you. You sense overwhelming danger in the gigantic stockpiles of arms and in the threats of nuclear war. You suffer when you see widespread hunger and malnutrition. You are concerned about the environment today and for the coming generations. You are threatened by unemployment, and many of you are already without work and without the prospect of meaningful employment. You are upset by the large number of people who are oppressed politically and spiritually and who cannot enjoy the exercise of their basic human rights as individuals or as a community. All this can give rise to a feeling that life has little meaning.

In this situation, some of you may be tempted to take flight from responsibility: in the fantasy worlds of alcohol and drugs, in shortlived sexual relationships without commitment to marriage and family, in indifference, in cynicism and even in violence. Put yourselves on guard against the fraud of a world that wants to exploit or misdirect your energetic and powerful search for happiness and meaning. But do not avoid the search for the true answers to the questions that confront you. Do not be afraid!

" The inevitable question: What is your idea of man?
Among the inevitable questions that you must ask yourselves, the first and foremost is this: What is your idea of man? What, to you, makes up the dignity and the greatness of a human being? This is a question that you young people have to ask yourselves but which you also put to the generation that has preceded you, to your parents and to all those who at various levels have had the responsibility of caring for the goods and values of the world. In the attempt to respond to this question honestly and openly, young and old can be led to reconsider their own actions and their own histories. Is it not true that very often, especially in the more developed and richer nations, people have given in to a materialistic idea of life? Is it not true that parents sometimes feel that they have fulfilled their obligations to their children by offering them, beyond the satisfaction of basic necessities, more material goods as the answer for their lives? Is it not true that, by doing this, they are passing on to the younger generations a world that will be poor in essential spiritual values, poor in peace and poor in justice? Is it not equally true that in other nations, the fascination with certain ideologies

15

has left to the younger generations a legacy of new forms of enslavement without the freedom to pursue the values that truly enhance life in all its aspects? Ask yourselves what kind of people you want yourselves and your fellow human beings to be, what kind of culture you want to build. Ask yourselves these questions and do not be afraid of the answers, even if they will require of you a change of direction in your thoughts and loyalties.

"The fundamental question: Who is your God?
The first question leads to an even more basic and fundamental one: Who is your God? We cannot define our notion of man without defining an Absolute, a fullness of truth, of beauty and of goodness by which we allow our lives to be guided. Thus it is true that a human being, "the visible image of the invisible God", cannot answer the question about who he or she is without at the same time declaring who his or her God is. It is impossible to restrict this question to the sphere of people's private existence. It is impossible to separate this question from the history of nations. Today, a person is exposed to the temptation to refuse God in the name of his or her own humanity. Wherever this refusal exists, there the shadow of fear casts its ever darkening pall. Fear is born wherever God dies in the consciences of human beings. Everyone knows, albeit obscurely and with dread, that wherever God dies in the conscience of the human person, there follows inevitably the death of man, the image of God."

Psalm 139

Yahweh, you examine me and know me,
you know when I sit, when I rise,
you understand my thoughts from afar.
You watch when I walk or lie down,
you know every detail of my conduct.

A word is not yet on my tongue
before you, Yahweh, know all about it.
You fence me in, behind and in front,
you have laid your hand upon me.
Such amazing knowledge is beyond me,
a height to which I cannot attain.

Where shall I go to escape your spirit?
Where shall I flee from your presence?
If I scale the heavens you are there,
if I lie flat in Sheol, there you are.

If I speed away on the wings of the dawn,
if I dwell beyond the ocean,
even there your hand will be guiding me,
your right hand holding me fast.

I will say, 'Let the darkness cover me,
and the night wrap itself around me,'
even darkness to you is not dark
and night is as clear as the day.

You created my innermost self,
knit me together in my mother's womb.
For so many marvels I thank you;
a wonder am I, and all your works are wonders.

You knew me through and through,
my being held no secrets from you,
when I was being formed in secret,
textured in the depths of the earth.

Your eyes could see my embryo.
In your book all my days were inscribed,
every one that was fixed is there.

How hard for me to grasp your thoughts,
how many, God, there are!
If I count them, they are more than the grains of the sand;
If I come to an end, I am still with you.

If only, God, you would kill the wicked! –
Men of violence, keep away from me! –
those who speak blasphemously about you,
and take no account of your thoughts.

Yahweh, do I not hate those who hate you,
and loathe those who defy you?
My hate for them has no limits,
I regard them as my own enemies.

God, examine me and know my heart,
test me and know my concerns.
Make sure that I am not on my way to ruin,
and guide me on the road to eternity.

The first dialogue
The son of the widow of Nain

Let us read together a page from the Gospels that invites us to ask ourselves *Who am I?* and *Who are You?* It is the story of the raising of the widow's son in Nain, narrated by the disciple Luke. Here is the literal translation from the Greek text:

> *We know that the 'he' referred to in this passage is Jesus, even though his name is not explicitly mentioned*

Resurrection of the widow's son in Nain (Lk: 7:11–17)

"It happened that soon afterwards he went to a town called Nain, accompanied by his disciples and a great number of people. Now when he was near the gate of the town there was a dead man being carried out, the only son of his mother, and she was a widow. And a considerable number of the townspeople were with her and, seeing her, the Lord was *deeply moved* and said to her, 'Do not go on crying.' Then he went up and touched the bier and the bearers stood still and he said, 'Young man, I say to you: wake up!' And the dead man sat up and began to talk, and Jesus gave him to his mother. Everyone was filled with awe and glorified God saying, 'A great prophet has risen up among us; God has visited his people. And this view of him spread throughout Judaea and all over the countryside."

As the central point of our reflection, consider the boy at that moment when he is called by Jesus. He gets up, looks into the eyes of Jesus and asks: "Who am I? Who are you?" In order to approach this central point of the story, we must begin by asking ourselves if we know of any other passages from the Gospels or the Bible which are similar to this passage and will therefore enable us to understand what it means.

How to look up a scripture reference

The name refers to the book of the Bible, Old or New Testament. If the name is an abbreviation, you can usually guess what it means. For example, Mk refers to Mark, the gospel of Mark. The first number is the chapter number. The next numbers are the verse numbers. So Lk 7:11–17 is Luke's gospel, chapter 7, verses 11 to 17. Matthew, Mark, Luke and John are often abbreviated to Mt, Mk, Lk & Jn respectively.

If the name of the book has a number before it, that means there are more than one book with the first name; 2Cor refers to the 2nd Letter of Paul to the Corinthians, for example.

Our first example of a story similar to the passage from Luke is the resurrection of Lazarus, as related by the disciple John (John 11:1–44). Here also we see Jesus confronted by the mystery of the life, death and new life of a person.

The gospel writer Mark tells us about the healing of the daughter of Jairus (Mark 5:21–43); this episode has parallels in certain details to the story in Luke (Luke 8:40–56). There is also a very moving passage in the Old Testament where the prophet Elijah is confronted by the death of a boy, the only son of the woman who has given him shelter (1 Kings 17:17–24). Having reminded ourselves of all these parallels, we can link the events in Nain, full of drama and rich in human potential, with other passages that illustrate the fundamental mysteries of existence (life and death) and which express an identical message: that Jesus is Lord of humanity and of life.

The power of the Resurrection

When we examine the passage more closely, we hear other resonances which place it in context within the entirety of Scripture. At verse 13, for example, Jesus' exhortation "Do not go on crying" (in Greek the verb *me kláie* is in the present imperative and therefore has a continuous meaning) reminds us of his questioning of Mary Magdalene after the Resurrection: "Woman, why are you still crying?" (*gúnai, ti kláieis;* John 20:13). The link with the risen Lord shows that Jesus is able to cope with human tears by means of the life force which is within him. Our text therefore confronts us with the strength and the energy which the Resurrection will bring to bear on the whole course of history.

> *In Luke's account of the miracle,*
> *he already realises the power Jesus*
> *has over life and death.*

Now we are able to understand another detail. At verse 13 Jesus is referred to as "Lord" (*Kúrios*). This title is used infrequently by the evangelists, who generally speak of "the Master" or "Jesus of Nazareth" or simply of "Jesus". The title "Lord" is typical of their proclamation of the kingship of Jesus, which is shown to be triumphant after his Resurrection. In Luke's account of the miracle, he already realises the power Jesus has over life and death. This is a text which expresses contemplation of the superior strength of Jesus over the greatest powers of historical reality.

The love of Jesus for humanity

In verse 13 we also read: "…seeing her, the Lord was deeply moved" (*kai idón autén o Kúrios esplanchnísthe*). The root of the Greek verb *esplanchnísthe*, is *splànchna*, and means "viscera, heart, guts". We could translate this literally as: 'he was moved in his guts'. Jesus was overtaken by an intense compassion because he was confronted by a person's most negative mystery: death. The same word is used in the parable of the Good Samaritan to express the power of conversion and of the Samaritan's approach to a stranger. The story of the Feeding of the Five Thousand tells us that Jesus, seeing the multitude, "was inwardly moved".

In the original ancient Greek version of the Prophecy of Zacharias (Luke 1:68–79) we find the Greek term *splànchna* again, *día splànchna eléus* (literally: through the guts or bowels of mercy) which can be translated as "Thanks be to the merciful goodness of our God". Here, therefore, the word denotes the passionate love of God for humankind, the profound compassion which Jesus has for us and which moves him to take care of each one of us.

The Epiphany of God's mercy

In the final part of our reading (verses 16 onwards) we can underline these lines: "Everyone was filled with awe and glorified God saying, 'God has visited his people.'" – *epesképsato o Theòs ton laòn autoù*. This echoes the Prophecy of Zacharias: "Blessed be the Lord God of Israel, for he has visited and redeemed his people."

> ***Epiphany*** *is a Greek word which means 'manifestation' or 'showing'. When the Magi come to see the infant Jesus, this is referred to as the Epiphany – Jesus is revealed as more than just an ordinary baby, as an infant king.*

According to Luke's account of the Nain episode, the people think about the Epiphany of the mercy of God: God who visits his people. It is, therefore, with a gaze full of faith that in these events they read the presence of God the creator and saviour of humankind.

I have only pointed out some of the resonances of our excerpt: if we were to undertake a comprehensive study, we would find that there are many more. This is the beauty of Scripture: each word and each line recalls others. Together, they all give us an idea of the greatness of God, who is revealed to us as we read these pages. Until now, however, we have only been doing preparatory work, seeing the story in the broader context of the Scriptures, in order to tune ourselves into the story of the widow of Nain's son. We can go on widening the context and then reflect on what we have found.

Meditating on the text: some questions

After having read and re-read this passage, we will try to meditate on it, asking some very simple questions about the story:

1. What did the boy say at the moment he came back to life? (This is the central point of our reflection.)
2. What did he experience?
3. What did Jesus say?
4. Why did Jesus say these words?
5. What do we say now and how do we want to live the power of this passage?

These are the five questions which I propose you ask yourselves. I shall suggest an answer to you and I want each one of you, personally, to develop it in greater depth.

1. *What did the boy say?*

We cannot tell from the excerpt, but there is a very interesting subtext from verse 15 onwards. The young man sat up "and began to talk". Note that it does not say that he began to move around or to exert himself. Why? Because speech, or the ability to express oneself, is a characteristic of a living, human personality. A person reaches maturity when he or she can express himself or herself, and talk, not while merely existing vegetatively or moving. The young man is introduced to us as someone to whom Jesus has restored language, the ability to communicate fully.

> *I think that when the boy looked at Jesus, he must have understood that he owed him everything; that he comprehended his creative power and that as a result he simply said to him: "Thank you, thank you Lord!"*

The author of the Gospel does not tell us what the boy said, because he wants us to imagine it: in this way the Bible is also a school of creativity. So I put myself in his situation, trying to live it with simplicity and sincerity. More than anything else, what comes into my mind is a word which I believe to be fundamental and which explains why the evangelist should have written that the young man "began to talk". I think that when he looked at Jesus, he must have understood that he owed him everything; that he comprehended his creative power and that as a result he simply said to him: "Thank you, thank you Lord!"

Here are the first words. Someone who has arrived at an awareness that they are loved by God, that they owe their life to him, and have received everything they have from him, exclaims: "Thank you, Lord!" The first answer to the questions: *Who am I ?* and *Who are you?* is that I am someone who has learnt to say 'thank you'.

To be more specific, I should express the first words like this: "Thank you, I owe you everything." It is at this point that I start to become truly aware of myself: when, looking into the eyes of the Lord, while praying, I manage to say with sincerity: "Thank you, my Lord. I owe you everything. You are the one who has given me life, speech, my being, my reason, movement, my parents, my home, my health, strength, and my weakness. I owe you everything."

> *"I thank God! I thank him for all he has given me! I thank him because he is everything to me."*

A personal story

A little while ago, on a pastoral visit to a parish on the outskirts of Milan, I went to see a young man, aged thirty-five. From the age of fourteen he had been in a wheelchair and subsequently bedridden. Paralysed and almost immobile, he could hardly speak and yet he said to me: "I thank God! I thank him for all he has given me! I thank him because he is everything to me." At a certain point he began to talk about chastity and was surprised that I found this strange. Now, however, I have realised the truth of what he was saying: for him chastity was the total gift of himself to God, it was his life given wholly to Jesus, without limits. Naturally I felt very lacking, faced by this young man who had managed to make such a complete gift and who lived through his illness without a word of recrimination! There was a great joy in his eyes, reserves of indescribable strength, and I said to myself: "Here is a person who has really known who God is for him. Here is someone who, in the presence of God, is able to say thank you!"

A few days later I was informed that this young man had died. I knew that he had communicated serenity to all the people who went to see him and that he had also encouraged vocations to the priesthood by saying, for example, to some of his friends: "Can't you see that you have been called by the Lord…look, this is what your life should be…"

I have told you about my meeting with that young man because in it I see the complete and correct answer to the questions: *Who am I? Who are you?*: "My God, you are everything to me and I offer you my life, just as it is, with its difficulties, because everything is in your hands." This is the first perception, the first dialogue on which a true personality can be built.

2. *What did the boy in Nain experience?*

Looking into Jesus' eyes, the boy experienced what it is to be really loved by God; he felt what it means to be understood, to be taken seriously, he understood what it means when we say that life is of value in the eyes of God.

> *I would like each one of you to practise saying this: "Lord, you understand me, you are the one who takes my life seriously. Sometimes I am in danger of gambling with my life. But you watch over me, because you made me, you created me, you gave me life. You see me in a way which makes me feel that I am taken seriously and am totally understood."*

It is difficult to feel that someone fully understands us, and sometimes we feel even our parents don't understand us. Often they do understand us, but there are still times when we cannot manage to explain ourselves. Only before the Lord can we say: "Lord, you are the one who totally understands me, you know who I am and you reveal yourself to me."

Let us try very hard to imagine what the boy experienced when he had been brought back to life and what each of us can experience when we know that we have been created and are valued by God, realising that our lives are willed by him through an act of creative love.

3. *What did Jesus say?*

The Gospel quotes three phrases spoken by Jesus at v. 14: "Young man, I tell you: get up!" The Scriptures never say anything without purpose and if three phrases are there, this is because there is an intention to express three things, a will to go more deeply into the way in which Jesus' relationship with us develops. "Young man" – this expression indicates that this is a boy like so many others: the son of a weeping widow, a member of a community, part of a people. Jesus engages with him within the framework of the boy's actual, physical surroundings, addressing himself to his social and cultural reality: "I tell you" – having made his approach to the boy in the wider context of his social, cultural and emotional background, Jesus then talks to him as an absolutely unique person: I am saying this to *you*.

"Get up" – this phrase, when it rings out in the New Testament, is a fanfare of resurrection. It means: *Live, there is a new life for you! There is a totally new possibility of life for you.*

The three phrases spoken by Jesus help us to answer the questions *Who am I?* and *Who are you?* I am, first and foremost, part of a very distinct family and social group. Each one of us is here because we are the children of our parents, part of a society, of a religious, cultural and human group. As such we are the objects of the love of God who calls us to him during the course of our lives.

> *"You, Lord, are the one who has loved me, has sought me out in this family, within relationships with my parents, brothers, sisters, relations, friends: people who share the immediate experience of my existence. You have wanted me and you love me within the context of my academic, cultural and social relationships."*

In these relationships as a whole there is, however, a personal and uncompromising phrase: "I say to you". And to no-one else. To understand who we ourselves are, we are asked to realise the singularity of our personal histories.

Our personal adventure is so unique that God has wanted it for its own sake and has not made it dependent on anyone else's. This constitutes the absolute dignity of my person: the fact that God wants me for myself. God therefore cares about the singularity of my life and my path, even if to me it seems to be of little interest, impoverished, modest. In God's mind and hands my utterly unique story is held, and God does not want to exchange it with that of anyone else. God does not want to exchange us with anyone because our value is definitive and irrevocable. Out of choice, God is irrevocably engaged in my personal history.

We seldom give much thought to this truth, not ascribing importance to ourselves, and yet this is the very source of our personal dignity. The roots and the origins of our being with others, of forming a community, of being creative, are in the phrase "I say to you!" While praying, it is important to glimpse, if for only an instant, the beauty of "I say to you!" "Lord, truly to me?" "Yes, indeed, to you!" "Truly, Lord, you who are great, infinite, you who have created the universe, you who have lived for ever and will live for ever, you say this to me?" "Yes, to you and for you!" We must never cease to be amazed by this truth! And we should then be able to understand the paralysed young man who on his deathbed exclaimed: "I thank you, my God, for all you have done for me!" He understood his life as a plan for him, and as love for him.

Let us now in prayer try to hear for ourselves the command "Arise": come back to life. "Oh Father, you pronounced this over me when you gave me life and created my soul, and you have repeated it lovingly, at the moment of my Baptism." In fact, for each of us this is the Baptismal word: "Arise, live the life of Christ, express the potential of your life." Who am I? I am the one who has been called in this way by God.

4. *Why did Jesus say these words?*

The reply to this and the following question I will leave for you to find, during personal reflection. I will confine myself to a brief suggestion.

Here the answer is in verse 13, in a word we have already discussed. For me God is tender and passionate love – God is passionate about me. We can meditate on this reality by slowly reciting the Lord's Prayer while thinking that God is Father to me because that is what God wants to be. And I? What am I for God?

5. *What are we to say now and how do we want to live the power of this text?*

You could recite verse 16: God has truly visited his people, he has visited each one of us, of you. We are the Epiphany of God. We should therefore learn to regard ourselves, and everyone else, as the mystery of God made manifest; we should reach that vision of faith which allows us to discern the revelation of God in history. Then our problems, difficulties, dislikes, problems with studying, weariness, boredom, bad weather, the day's gloomier moments, illness, everything, in fact, will reveal to us the presence of God in our lives. This is what it means to know who I am. I am a miracle of God, in whom he reveals himself as my personal history unfolds.

And Who, Lord, are you? You are the one who says: "To you. I am talking to you! Live your life to the full and do not be afraid, do not be fearful. It does not matter that you believe you are not very gifted, that you do not know how to do this or that, because I am with you and this is your life!"

The second dialogue
A difficult and liberating dialogue

"My God, I thank you! You are everything to me,"

In the preceding meditation we looked at the first dialogue, the fundamental exchange of words through which we place ourselves in truth before God by saying: "My God, I thank you! You are everything to me," and God responds: "Live! Wake up! To work!"

Such a dialogue is, however, not always easy: it is sometimes obstructed by difficulties of various kinds. For this reason, during this meditation we want to have a better understanding of who we are; of who I am as a partner in a conversation which is often complicated and tortuous. We entrust ourselves to the protection of Mary, mother of the Lord, wanting to progress towards total liberty and maturity in our dialogue with God.

The Gospel story which we will be reflecting on is about a boy who finds himself in a very fraught relationship with Jesus. Even the apostles were unable to initiate dialogue with him, and all the strength of the Lord was to prove necessary. We will read the passage, trying to grasp the mystery it contains and its significance for humankind in every era. The story is related in the three Synoptic Gospels, and we have chosen the version in Mark 9:14–29. It is a fairly difficult text, even in Greek, because of the presence of new terms: indeed, the vocabulary could be described as a challenge in itself.

The healing of the epileptic (Mk 9:14–29)

"As they were rejoining the disciples they saw a large crowd round them and some scribes arguing with them. At once, when they saw him, the whole crowd were struck with amazement and ran to greet him. And the asked them, 'What are you arguing about with them?' A man answered him from the crowd, 'Master, I have brought my son to you; there is a spirit of dumbness in him, and when it takes hold of him it throws him to the ground, and he foams at the mouth and grinds his teeth and goes rigid. And I asked your disciples to drive it out and they were unable to.'

In reply he said to them, 'Faithless generation, how much longer must I be among you? How much longer must I put up with you? Bring him to me.' They brought the boy to him, and at once the spirit of dumbness threw the boy into convulsions, and he fell to the ground and lay writhing there, foaming at the mouth. Jesus asked the father, 'How long has this been happening to him?' 'From childhood,' he said, and it has often thrown him into fire and into water, in order to destroy him. But if you can do anything, have pity on us and help us.' 'If you can?' retorted Jesus. 'Everything is possible for one who has faith.' At once the father of the boy cried out, 'I have faith. Help my lack of faith!'

And when Jesus saw that a crowd was gathering, he rebuked the unclean spirit. 'Deaf and dumb spirit,' he said, 'I command you: come out of him and never enter him again.' Then it threw the boy into violent convulsions and came out shouting, and the boy lay there so like a corpse that most of them said, 'He is dead.' But Jesus took him by the hand and helped him up, and he was able to stand. When he had gone indoors, his disciples asked him when they were by themselves, 'Why were we unable to drive it out?' He answered, 'This is the kind that can be driven out only by prayer.'"

The passage is very long. I would like to make just one comment on the context, without pointing out parallel passages, which you can do for yourself. My comment is that in all three Gospels this passage comes after the story of the Transfiguration, which means after Jesus has revealed himself in glory.

Coming down from the mountain, Jesus came towards a large crowd and the people were astonished, exclaiming: "But where has he come from? He wasn't here before!" They all ran towards him and explained the problem to him. The reader of the Gospel, who has realised from the episode of the Transfiguration what inner power Jesus has, can now easily recognise his power over people, over each one of us. This is the connection between the two questions *Who am I?* and *Who are You?*

Discovering that you are powerful and great, Lord, I also know who I am, I see my difficulties and my problems more clearly, which you, can solve.

In order to reflect on the passage in the spirit of a dialogue, I invite you to consider three aspects of it briefly:

1. This boy and his enemies, as obstacles to the dialogue;
2. The help which is gradually given to the boy;
3. His release from epilepsy.

Obstacles to the dialogue

The boy – says the evangelist when describing him – has, first of all, a mute spirit, which means he cannot express himself. Note the psychological insight of these pages of the Gospel. In the episode of the widow of Nain's son, the first thing the resuscitated boy did was to talk. Jesus restored his personal power to him through speech itself. But the epileptic's power of expression is blocked. So the greater misfortune, which touches us most closely, is for our power of expression to be impeded.

The enemy of humankind wants us to be incapable of growth and wants us to be blocked and closed, to become incapable of expressing ourselves, of talking with God and with our brothers and sisters. This is, perhaps, the quintessence of the Devil's cunning and strategy, especially in the case of a boy whose personality is developing. The intention of the adversary is precisely this: to halt human development in various ways, so that, shut up within themselves, they will become sad, lazy, egotistical, greedy, sensual, given over to pleasure, incapable of true openness. Here we are really touching on the fundamental problem of the formation of a person.

When we observe this boy more closely, we see that the Gospel introduces him to us in three stages. At v. 17 he is *someone who does not speak*. At v. 18 we are told that he is *possessed*, that he therefore has violent changes of mood: he moves about jerkily, gets agitated, foams at the mouth, grinds his teeth, and becomes rigid. The passage dramatically describes a person in thrall to his emotions and inner tensions, incapable of giving them outward expression. Finally, at v. 20 and then at v. 22, he is shown to us as someone who has a mania for inflicting injury upon himself: he is *self-destructive*, throwing himself into water or fire. People with some kinds of mental illness can sometimes be seen behaving in a similar way: they want to injure themselves, banging their heads against the walls and trying to hurt themselves.

> *These are three successive phases in the disintegration of a person and in this passage they are described in their pathological forms.*

These are three successive phases in the disintegration of a person and in this passage they are described in their pathological forms. They are, however, metaphors illustrating behavioural patterns which, at a more subtle level, amount to the opposite of a dialogue with God and with others. The Scriptures therefore invite us to examine these traits, which are shown to be very dangerous because they undermine our comprehension of ourselves and of God and because they prevent us from understanding who we are and who God is. We will now try to go into more detail about the three obstacles which we have identified.

a) *Blocked self-expression*

Blocked self-expression is the clearest indication in us of failure in personality development. Basically, training as students consists of learning to say exactly what you think. Study of the great classical authors, of literature, mathematics, history, are all ways of acquiring that richness of language with which people have expressed themselves. Unfortunately, there are still all too many adults who cannot progress beyond the use of just three or four phrases in their everyday life. Even though they may watch television and listen to the radio, their expressive capacity remains restricted. This is a block which should not exist, because we are all made to be capable of assimilating a diversity of values and to be able to demonstrate this freely and openly.

> *All your hard work studying so many subjects is, of course, directed at learning particular truths but, most importantly, at acquiring that ability which has been given to you to express yourselves and the realities of your lives, drawing upon a wealth of imagery and effective language.*

It is interesting to trace the progressive development of the ability to achieve a synthesis of meaning in a child and subsequently in a young adult, from the age of ten to twenty. It grows as his or her mastery of vocabulary increases, together with the capacity to match feelings to words and modes of expression. Education plays an important part in this. All your hard work studying so many subjects is, of course, directed at learning particular truths but, most importantly, at acquiring that ability which has been given to you to express yourselves and the realities of your lives, drawing upon a wealth of imagery and effective language.

Why do we admire great writers such as, to take just one example, Manzoni? Because he possesses such richness of expression. Turning the pages of his books, as we read his words we see the human heart emerge, the souls of people not only of his time but of any era. For example, when I, as a bishop, read the pages about Cardinal Federigo and his talks with Don Abbondio, I recognise myself, my desires, my fears. This is richness of expression, a sign of human and Christian maturity.

Naturally our enemy tells us: "But no, this isn't necessary. You only need a few words, a few notions, a few concepts." He wants us to shun the effort of full and accurate expressiveness. You must know some young people who talk in monosyllables, use slang, repeat certain slogans. They are incapable of talking about anything more than two or three subjects.

> *The subjects you are studying are nothing less than the communication of deep intuitions which humanity has had about nature, history and science, which you should accept as a resource for expression.*

Humanity develops through richness of speech. Naturally our manner of speaking varies: we have different gifts, which grow with time. I remember when I was young, I found public speaking an ordeal: I was nervous and apt to become tongue-tied. It takes time to develop skill. Effort is important, however, and is a requirement for the acquisition of knowledge. I urge you, therefore, to experience your educational life both as a means of knowing yourselves and of cultivating an ability to communicate with the largest possible number of people. The subjects you are studying are nothing less than the communication of deep intuitions which humanity has had about nature, history and science, which you should accept as a resource for expression.

b) *Lack of discipline in feelings and emotions*

The second obstacle concerns *lack of discipline in feelings and emotions*. The dumb spirit – says the Gospel – grabbed hold of the boy and threw him to the ground, where he lay foaming at the mouth, grinding his teeth and becoming rigid.

What aspect of myself can I understand when I think about this behaviour? Any of those aspects which are revealed in my daily life every time my feelings and emotions run riot inside me and which, if I do not find a means of expressing them properly and accurately, will create a blockage and provoke tension. I may not be aware that I am inwardly cramped by them: their symptoms are indifference, tiredness, ill humour, laziness, stress, loss of enthusiasm.

These negative attitudes are so often caused by emotional disorder within us! It is therefore important to understand "who I am", what are the deepest emotions which frighten me or which make me retreat into myself. It is not easy to attain this insight and yet it is indispensable, especially for those who, in their everyday lives, are to be responsible for others. One of the requirements which the spiritual fathers of the Eastern church impressed upon any pupil who wanted to embark on a monastic life or Christian discipleship was this: "Put your thoughts, your fantasies and your emotions in order! If you fail to do this, they will throw you into confusion, upset and hurt you, drive you in opposing directions and you will be left, without realising it, bereft of strength!"

How do we put our feelings in order? Their existence is not necessarily harmful, but they usually emerge in a disorderly manner. We need to learn to examine ourselves. I will point out four things which you need to look at in yourselves.

Imagination. You can ask yourselves: where do my thoughts go when they are allowed to roam freely?

Likes and *dislikes*. The latter often arise unexpectedly, perhaps when someone has offended us or treated us with discourtesy. If I do not carry out a thorough self-examination, antipathy tends to become permanent.

Emotions. Our *emotions* can sometimes well up unexpectedly, without us realising it. It is important to be aware of them so that we can get them into perspective.

Bad temper. Why am I in a bad mood? Perhaps because it is raining. If I understand that this is the reason, I get things into perspective and say to myself: "Don't worry, it's just a passing bit of bad temper." I can see a reason for what I am going through.

> *A mature person normally lives his
> or her emotions and feelings
> realistically, as they relate to
> things, relationships, people,
> responsibilities.*

The entire journey from adolescence to adulthood depends on this progressive capacity to examine, dominate, instil order in my imagination, likes and dislikes, emotionalism, excessive enthusiasms, indifference. We begin to get to know ourselves better, to understand that the dialogue with ourselves and our dialogue with Jesus is blocked each time we let ourselves be dominated by these attributes and emotional conditions. Obviously we do not have to try to eradicate them, because we shall always have emotions and feelings. These are what make human beings so rich: but a mature person normally lives his or her emotions and feelings realistically, as they relate to things, relationships, people, responsibilities.

c) *Self-destructiveness*
The third obstacle, which is more difficult to understand, is *self-destructiveness.* There are situations where we also become somewhat self-destructive. We feel guilty without any justification, we sabotage ourselves, we become disheartened, almost enjoying our discouragement. We cannot be perfect, better than anyone else, so we take pleasure in being the worst and in being worthless. It is all down to pride.

If someone happens not to smile when they look at us, doesn't say hello immediately, we think that they are annoyed with us; if someone tells us off when it isn't fully justified, we think ourselves unfairly and badly treated and we become resentful. We are at the lowest level, when all the forms of temptation are mobilised to try to depress us, to weigh us down, to clip our wings. While the uncontrolled interplay of emotions was the main problem in our second obstacle, here it is more of a sign of evil. The Devil suggests to us: "You can't help it, you'll give in, you can't resist temptation." Sometimes we do succumb to evil almost as if to justify our resentment or rage. We allow ourselves be deceived and we block our dialogue which should always take place when we are in a state of joy, serenity, peace and in control of ourselves.

> *The image of the epileptic boy provides us with an illustration of the three successive phases: inarticulateness, rigidity, and repressed rage. These stand for what is most harmful to our ability to answer the questions Who am I? Who are You?*

The image of the epileptic boy provides us with an illustration of the three successive phases: inarticulateness, rigidity, and repressed rage. These stand for what is most harmful to our ability to answer the questions *Who am I? Who are You?* In such a situation it is extremely difficult to discern a vocation, to understand what forces for good exist in a person.

> *Maturity does not consist in closing your eyes to situations but in learning to manage your troublesome humanity.*

You should now set about exploring in greater depth the obstacles which I have described. Perhaps you may say: "No, they have nothing to do with me. I have a good-natured, sweet-tempered, peaceable and serene character, always cheerful…and I thank God for it." I believe, however, that many of you (and this has also happened to me) will have experienced moments in which you realise that in your innermost selves there are various deep and difficult layers, which you must learn to control. Maturity does not consist in closing your eyes to situations but in learning to manage your troublesome humanity.

Who am I? Not a saint or even a person who lives an angelic life; I am someone who lives through some easy moments and some difficult moments and I must learn to master my difficulties rationally and in the spirit of faith. Then I shall be able to grow up within a dialogue which becomes recognition of who I am, and of who God is for me, and which will enable me to understand what I must do with my life.

The help that was gradually given to the boy

Let us try to see from our reading how the boy in our story was helped. I am selecting three words, which you will then look for in the narrative: explanation, objectivity, and belief.

Explanation: the poor boy is incapable of anything, but his father is there to help him, to stand in for him and to identify his needs. First of all, he needs to explain what is happening. If the father had withdrawn into himself, saying: "There he is, heal him," he would not have got anywhere. This parent, however, clarifies the situation, makes an effort to have a dialogue, to communicate. It is therefore necessary for us to learn how to show ourselves as we are, to declare ourselves.

> *I advise you young people and, in general, anyone who cannot have any spiritual direction, to make your Confession in the form of a penitential dialogue.*

I advise you young people and, in general, anyone who cannot have any spiritual direction, to make your Confession in the form of a penitential dialogue. Not just to tell your obvious sins but also your dislikes, fears, bad moods, strong dislikes. I repeat: we must learn to tell all about ourselves, to enter into a dialogue, try to reveal ourselves, explaining ourselves with trust, knowing that Jesus is listening to us, that he loves us and wants us to know ourselves.

Objectivity: when Jesus hears the father's explanation, he asks: "How long has this been going on?" He makes him give a complete picture of the situation, seeking to extricate him from the anxiety he is experiencing at that moment. Jesus tries to place what is happening to the boy in the context of his entire life.

We need to distance ourselves from ourselves, from our faults, our troubles, our difficulties. In other words, we have to be objective. Therefore it's sensible to say: "Let's see what is happening to me: perhaps it is due to tiredness, stress, perhaps a disappointment at school, with a friend, perhaps it is because of a criticism…" We make a list of our difficulties, aiming to write them all down, we consider the situation point by point. Once we have distanced ourselves, we no longer feel that we are drowning. We realise that we are in a certain state of mind and we say: "If this is how I am, it means that the Lord – who certainly loves me – has a plan for me – to make me take a path which I do not yet know but which he knows. I will try to understand this path." This is how we progress towards maturity.

> *Taking steps in the direction of self-knowledge does not mean being perfect or never making mistakes.*

Taking steps in the direction of self-knowledge does not mean being perfect or never making mistakes; it does not mean never being bad-tempered or depressed. Instead it means that we learn to be objective and mature about the difficulties which we encounter and come to the conclusion: "This is how I feel now. How can I manage these difficulties before God?"

Belief is the third word. This is the way in which Jesus brings us to say: "Only believe…" We too must say: "Lord, I trust you, for the very reason that I am as I am, that I have discovered that I am like this. I know that you are my saviour."

You will realise that the question *Who are You?*, has now acquired a new depth. "You are not only the one who has granted me life and given me possibilities.

You are also the one who gives me your hand and leads me through my everyday worries. You will make sure that I do not give in to temptation. You help me out of my difficulties."

> *True knowledge of the Lord is so precious that the Lord sometimes leaves us full of faults, allowing us to have shortcomings and to make mistakes; then we can receive this knowledge of ourselves and say in faith, "Lord, I believe in you!"*

I truly know Jesus when I understand him as the one who frees me from the shackles, the darkness, the wretchedness of life; as the one who comes to me not only when I am loving towards him or full of enthusiasm but also when I am utterly depressed. I know that Jesus is with me to say to me: "I am your salvation." True knowledge of the Lord is so precious that the Lord sometimes leaves us full of faults, allowing us to have shortcomings and to make mistakes; then we can receive this knowledge of ourselves and say in faith, "Lord, I believe in you!"

The release from epilepsy

At verse 25 Jesus says: "You deaf and dumb spirit, I charge you, come out of him, and enter no more into him." This is the meeting with Jesus the liberator. "Lord, you are my liberator, you are my salvation. You are the one who rehabilitates me, who makes me a real person. You enable me to express myself and take control of my negative realities. You are my saviour." Here is the knowledge of Jesus which we must attain; this is the dialogue which we must achieve.

I leave you to continue your reflections on these aspects of the passage and I suggest we end by reading a prayer of St Ambrose:

Christ is everything to us.
If you have a wound which needs healing, he is the doctor;
If you burn with fever, he is the fountain;
If you are oppressed, he is justice;
If you need help, he is strength;
If you desire heaven, he is the way;
If you fear death, he is life;
If you are afraid of the dark, he is light;
If you seek food, he is nourishment.

The third dialogue
The love which saves

The love which saves
First Reading: Genesis 50:15–21

Seeing that their father was dead, Joseph's brothers said, 'What if Joseph intends to treat us as enemies and pay us back for all the wrong we did him?' So they sent this message to Joseph: 'Before your father died, he gave us this order: "You are to say to Joseph: Now please forgive the crime and faults of your brothers and all the wrong they did you." So now please forgive the crime of the servants of your father's God.' Joseph wept at the message they sent to him.

Then his brothers went to him themselves and, throwing themselves at his feet, said, 'Take us as your slaves!' But Joseph replied, 'Do not be afraid; is it for me to put myself in God's place? The evil you planned to do me has by God's design been turned to good, to bring about the present result: the survival of a numerous people. So there is no need to be afraid; I shall provide for you and your dependents.' In this way he reassured them by speaking affectionately to them.

Second Reading: Proverbs 3:27–35

Refuse no kindness to those who have a right to it,
if it is in your power to perform it.
Do not say to your neighbour, 'Go away! Come another time!
I will give it to you tomorrow,' if you can do it now.
Do not plot harm against your neighbour

who is living unsuspecting beside you.
Do not pick a groundless quarrel with anyone
who has done you no harm.
Do not envy the man of violence,
never model your conduct on his;
for the wilful wrong-doer is abhorrent to Yahweh,
who confides only in the honest.
Yahweh's curse lies on the house of the wicked,
but he blesses the home of the upright.
He mocks those who mock,
but accords his favour to the humble.
Glory is the portion of the wise,
all that fools inherit is contempt.

Gospel Reading: Matthew 5:38–48

'You have heard how it was said: *Eye for eye and tooth for tooth.* But I say this to you: offer no resistance to the wicked. On the contrary, if anyone hits you on the right cheek, offer him the other as well; if someone wishes to go to law with you to get your tunic, let him have your cloak as well. And if anyone requires you to go one mile, go two miles with him. Give to anyone who asks you, and if anyone wants to borrow, do not turn away.

You have heard how it was said, You will love your neighbour and hate your enemy. But I say this to you, love your enemies and pray for those who persecute you; so that you may be children of your Father in heaven, for he causes his sun to rise on the bad as well as the good, and sends down rain to fall on the upright and the wicked alike. For if you love those who love you, what reward will you get? Do not even the tax collectors do as much? And if you save your greetings for your brothers, are you doing anything exceptional? Do not even the gentiles do as much? You must therefore set no bounds to your love, just as your heavenly Father sets none to his.'

The readings we have listened to have the same key words as that found in the parable of the Good Samaritan, which I touched upon in my Pastoral Letter *Draw near* and which we have also found in the story of the widow of Nain's son: *He was deeply moved*, from the Greek *esplanchnìsthe*.

This concerns the deep compassion which the Samaritan has for his neighbour; the intense compassion of Jesus when confronted by the dead boy; the profound compassion of God for humanity, which we are invited to imitate in the passage from Matthew's gospel, "You must therefore be perfect, just as your heavenly Father is perfect."

The Father is the one who loves us deeply and his love is at the root of the admonitions about charity which we have heard from the Book of Proverbs. The love of the Father is also the literary and dramatic key to the passage from Genesis, on which I will comment briefly.

The lamentation of Joseph

"Joseph wept…." This scene describes the most intense compassion. *Why did Joseph burst into tears?* Joseph was the favourite child of Jacob. Envied by his brothers, he was betrayed and condemned to death, then sold to slave dealers and taken to Egypt. Joseph, however, welcomes these brothers, who have done him so much harm, with open arms. Here our questions *Who am I? Who are You?* achieve an amazingly concrete reality.

> *Joseph weeps because he feels misunderstood, because his brothers do not believe him and do not trust him.*

I – says Joseph – am someone with a big heart, who can forgive and not bear a grudge. And you are the ones who must believe in my capacity for forgiveness. Doubts arise, however, which challenge Joseph's response. The brothers do not believe that Joseph has forgiven them, they do not wholly trust him, they are not convinced that someone can really totally forgive when they have been so grievously wronged. And so, when their father dies, they become anxious and fearful and would have Joseph believe that their father said: "…forgive the crime and faults of your brothers." Joseph weeps because he feels misunderstood, because his brothers do not believe him and do not trust him.

Here we see how difficult it is to answer our questions *Who am I? Who are You?*, even when "You" is the Lord. Instinctively we create an idea of Jesus as someone who understands us but who, after a certain point, grows weary of us, as we grow weary of ourselves. Each time we feel lazy or discouraged, we have the impression that even God can no longer count on us. We have disappointed God and we think that, through our fault, our relationship with God is broken.

This means that we do not know the Lord, we do not trust the Lord, we have not understood who the Lord is. We could be different, full of comfort and joy, as the Joseph story suggests: "He reassured them by speaking affectionately to them." To understand who the Lord is, to manage to achieve a true act of recognition, is to feel that we are appreciated by God for what we are as well as being valued for what we could be.

This dual knowledge is therefore very important: *that I should know myself and that I should know God and know that I am known by God*. This is the root of everything. When this knowledge is flawed, what befell Joseph's brothers happens us: we are overcome by fear, dread, suspicion, anxiety. We mistrust Jesus, we mistrust others, we mistrust the Church.

Prayer

For those who know Jesus, prayer is the continuous channel through which this living knowledge can be deepened. And we are spending these days in order to grow in this relationship and reach the stage where we can truly say:

> "Lord, you know me, I know you and I know that you know me. I
> rely on the knowledge which you have of me in order to know

myself. We are here together to fulfil this act of knowledge of you. You place the mystery of your death in our hands. It is no small thing that you should entrust us with the mystery of your Body and of your Blood. Lord, you entrust it to our very frail hands! How can you place such a precious treasure in the hands of careless and feckless people, whose thoughts often wander, even during Mass? How can you, Lord?"

And the Lord answers us: "I know you, I trust you and I grant you trust. I want you to know me as the one who trusts you to the depths of your being."

We must experience this Eucharist as a gesture of limitless trust in which Jesus, the Son of God, places his body in our hands and says: "Do what you will." There is no greater act of trust! Remember the words of Joseph to his brothers: "I am here: if you trust me, do not be afraid."

"Lord, make us recognise you in this Eucharist. Grant that this celebration be a step forward in understanding who I am: someone greatly loved by you. And who are you? You are the one who places in my hands his Body and his Blood, a person therefore who is more important for me than anyone else I could imagine."

Mutual love

> *"Make us all, O Lord, recognise one another as brothers and look into one another's hearts."*

Jesus makes himself known by giving himself. This is a reality which reminds us of the mutual love which we must live in the Church. Sometimes the newspapers emphasise differences of opinion that exist within the Church, which seem to reflect the mutual fears of Joseph's brothers. It is, however, the Lord's will that when Christians are gathered together they admit that they are all needful of forgiveness, they are all sinners and all loved by God, ready to trust one another. "Make us all, O Lord, recognise one another as brothers and look into one another's hearts."

"Grant that we may feel that we all have the same gift of reconciliation, of mercy and forgiveness that you have placed in the soul of each person and which you are about to instil in our inner selves through this Eucharist."

A great and difficult task

"I thank you, Father, because over and above the things which we can or cannot do, over and above our ability or inability to pray, you are with us and will never abandon us. We thank you because you are the one who guides our reflections during these days, and our exercises in prayer. We are often inattentive when undertaking these exercises, we approach them lazily and with reluctance. Perhaps we do want to pray and yet we are full of inertia. But you, Father, are always full of love and attention. We thank you, we praise you and we bless you for being like this and we ask you for the grace to follow a true path of prayer. Help us to rein in our imaginations and gather our thoughts, so that we can concentrate while we are in your presence. Help us also to make a sacrifice of our bodies which are sometimes rebellious; help us to offer this physical sacrifice in order to live in an attitude of prayer.

Receive, Lord, what little I have to give: my body present before you and trying to pray coherently. Above all, I ask you, O Father, to rekindle in me the fire of faith, so that I will be able to feel the living force of your presence as Father. I ask you this for the sake of Jesus, your Son, who prayed at night; on the mountain; in the early morning; while walking the roads of Palestine; in the Temple.

You, Jesus, prayed everywhere, even on the cross; enter into us with your spirit of prayer. O Jesus, who lives in Mary, enter into us, your servants, and grant us your spirit of adoration. Render our hearts full of peace so that we can pray with you and in the same way as you."

One of the typical fruits of a retreat such as this is a new ability to pray, and we should therefore experience the time spent on our reflections as an exercise in prayer.

The fourth dialogue
The ability to pray
David, shepherd and king

The character on whom we are now about to meditate, praying for help in answering the question which has provided the theme of our retreat, is David: or, rather, some aspects of David's personality specifically mentioned in the First Book of Samuel.

We could call this meditation *David at War* because David has been called to a great and difficult task, greater than his own strength. First we will ask ourselves:

1. Who have you chosen, Lord? (referring to I Samuel 16:6–13)
2. Then we will think about David's assertion that he comes in the name of the Lord. (I Samuel 17:32–51)
3. Finally we will reflect on his declaration that the Lord has given him victory. (Psalm 18 is our commentary on the story of David)

These are therefore variations on our theme questions, *Who am I? Who are You?*

Who have you chosen, Lord?

> *Bethlehem will be the birthplace of Jesus, and consequently in the figure of David we already glimpse the Messiah, Jesus Christ; this does not, however, seem to mark the germination of the mystery which will be revealed later.*

The prophet Samuel arrives in the city of Bethlehem. Samuel summons a family from Bethlehem, the family of Jesse, and says to Jesse: "I want to make a sacrifice." He then makes his wish known to the entire city; he makes

Jesse and his sons prepare for the rite and invites them to the ceremony. We shall now read the passage I Samuel 16:6ff

> "When they arrived, he looked at Eliab and thought, 'This must be Yahweh's anointed now before him, 'but Yahweh said to Samuel, 'Take no notice of his appearance or his height, for I have rejected him; God does not see as human beings see; they look at appearances but Yahweh looks at the heart.' Jesse then called Abinadab and presented him to Samuel, who said, 'Yahweh has not chosen this one either.' Jesse then presented Shammah, but Samuel said, 'Yahweh has not chosen this one either.'

> Jesse thus presented seven of his sons to Samuel, but Samuel said to Jesse, 'Yahweh has not chosen these.' He then asked Jesse, 'Are these all the sons you have?' Jesse replied, 'There is still one left, the youngest; he is looking after the sheep.' Samuel then said to Jesse, 'Send for him, for we shall not sit down to eat until he arrives.' Jesse had him sent for; he had ruddy cheeks, with fine eyes and an attractive appearance. Yahweh said, 'Get up and anoint him: he is the one!'

> At this, Samuel took the horn of oil and anointed him, surrounded by his brothers; and the spirit of Yahweh seized on David from that day onwards. Samuel, for his part, set off and went to Ramah."

Regarding this passage, we can ask, "Who have you chosen, Lord?" I will give the answer in the form of two statements.

David did not become proud

First of all *David did not become proud*. What does this mean? He was certainly aware, even though he was outside the city of Bethlehem at the time, that a great prophet had arrived; he knew that he had gone to his home and had started to summon his brothers one by one. We might think that David would have been filled with envy and resentment: "Why has he not called me? But who am I? They scorn me because I am the last. They do not even let me see the prophet! They are enjoying themselves and they leave me alone in the countryside to take care of the sheep..."

> *David is a serene boy because he can live his daily life trusting in God, like Jesus of Nazareth, who grew in wisdom, stature and grace day by day in divine peace and in the anticipation of God's chosen moment.*

From the story, however, we realise that David gives himself no airs, he has no pretensions, he gets on with whatever he is asked to do, saying: "The Lord will take care of me." David is not egotistical, quarrelsome, preoccupied with himself. He lives his daily life with simplicity, and can find the will of God wherever it may be, a day at a time. He therefore stays where he is and continues to get on quietly with his work, even though he has heard what is happening at home. Although he knows his own worth, David is a serene boy because he can live his daily life trusting in God, like Jesus of Nazareth, who grew in wisdom, stature and grace day by day in divine peace and in the anticipation of God's chosen moment.

David does not draw back

This facet of David's character corresponds with another: *he does not draw back*. This is the strange thing about this story: while his older brothers are being examined to see who is the one chosen to be anointed king, representing political power, David does not give any thought to it. But when he is called he responds naturally and without hesitation; he does not draw back.

The same strength which enabled him to live each day with such simplicity becomes a willingness to accept a task which places him above his older brothers. Confronted with a serious responsibility, he accepts this as a gift from the Holy Spirit: "...the spirit of Yahweh seized on David from that day onwards." He knows very well that he is the least, and is convinced that he cannot expect anything. However, when the Spirit of the Lord is conferred upon him, he receives it with total trust.

> *When the Spirit of the Lord is conferred upon him, David receives it with total trust.*

For us the question arises: Who am I compared with David? Who am I? Am I not at risk of being resentful or worried when it seems that I have been overlooked, or of becoming proud and unbending when I find myself at the centre of things?

During your private meditation, I suggest you look for parallels of this peace. The most beautiful example which occurs to me is to be found in the first chapter of Luke's gospel in the account of the angel's Annunciation to Mary. Mary is not filled with pride. The extraordinary event which is happening to her is an unexpected grace of which she does not believe herself worthy: "But what is this? Why me? Why? What is it to do with me?" With the same simplicity as David, however, she does not draw back: "You see before you the Lord's servant, let it happen to me as you have said."

Here we grasp the total commitment of a vocation which is born of simplicity: "Lord, I know that I cannot aspire to anything. I am content that you should love me as I am and if you call me, Lord, I am ready."

> *"Lord, grant that I may enter into that peace which comes from placing my life in your hands!"*

The question *Who have you chosen, Lord?* meets with the coherent reply: *You have chosen someone who seemed much less capable than others but who had a simple heart and a readiness to serve you without ambition.*

Sometimes we compare ourselves with others who are much better than us, and who do not seem to have the calling which has been offered to us; we have to ask the Lord with great humility why he has chosen us. He has chosen us not because we are particularly clever or brilliant but because he loves us.

"Lord, I want to thank you and ask you for the grace to trust in you, and not to draw back. Grant, O Lord, that I should not refuse but that I place myself simply in your hands." This is the prayer that we can say to accompany the passage to which we have given the title *Who have you chosen, Lord?*

I come in the strength of the Lord

Now we can read, in I Samuel 17:32-39, the story of how David challenged Goliath, the man whom nobody dared to confront:

> "David said to Saul, 'Let no one be discouraged on his account; your servant will go and fight this Philistine.' Saul said to David, 'You cannot go and fight the Philistine; you are only a boy and he has been a warrior since his youth.'
>
> David said to Saul, 'Your servant used to look after the sheep for his father and whenever a lion or a bear came and took a sheep from the flock, I used to follow it up, lay into it and snatch it out of its jaws. If it turned on me, I would seize it by the beard and batter it to death. Your servant has killed both lion and bear, and this uncircumcised Philistine will end up like one of them for having challenged the armies of the living God.' 'Yahweh,' David went on, 'who delivered me from the claws of lion and bear, will deliver me from the clutches of this Philistine.' Then Saul said to David, 'God, and Yahweh be with you!'
>
> Saul dressed David in his own armour; he put a bronze helmet on his head, dressed him in a breastplate and buckled his own sword over David's armour. David tried to walk but, not being used to them, said to Saul, 'I cannot walk in these; I am not used to them.' So they took them off again."

David's ability

Let us consider *David's ability*. He knows he is strong and capable but when he has put on Saul's armour he admits that he cannot manage to fight in it. If he had been vain and proud, he would have said: "What are you talking about? What do you mean? Dressed in the king's armour, of course I shall manage! I must wear this armour because that is what a strong man does!" David, however, while knowing his own worth, refuses to mind about those outward appearances which signified strength.

> *Authenticity, or being true to oneself, is a fundamental virtue: it is the courage to be ourselves in our positive and negative aspects, in the talents which we possess and also in the limitations which each one of us also has.*

I discern *great authenticity* in David. He really knows himself, he is aware of what he can do and what he cannot do. Authenticity, or being true to oneself, is a fundamental virtue: it is the courage to be ourselves in our positive and negative aspects, in the talents which we possess and also in the limitations which each one of us also has. Yet it is very difficult to be authentic in a competitive society like ours, in which some are successful, and manage to acquire power over others – cultural and moral power as well as economic power.

The temptation is always not to be ourselves but rather to imitate successful people. This gives rise to hero worship – we copy the most popular pop singer, footballer, film star or politician.

It is true there can be a good side to emulating someone. But all too often a subtle deception underlies this; knowing that I do not amount to much, I try to identify, if only in my imagination, with a particular actor, singer or politician.

My fantasies make me identify with that person and I reject the simple truth and strength of my life.

We can fall into this particular little trap even where the saints are concerned. There is a way of looking at the saints which is not helpful to our growth, but illusory. We would like to be what we are not, and imagination makes us believe we are different from our own truth; it makes us confuse the enthusiasm we feel for, say, Francis of Assisi or for Charles de Foucauld with the reality of our being.

> *We are called upon to be authentic in certain simple and true things, to find inspiration in great men and women, not to delude ourselves but to help us walk in the way of truth.*

David, however, did not think he was a great warrior just because he had put on the armour of the king: he admitted that it was not suitable for him. We are called upon to be authentic in certain simple and true things, to find inspiration in great men and women, not to delude ourselves but to help us walk in the way of truth.

I very much admire the great mountaineers and I enjoy looking at photographs of them tackling rock faces rated grade six in difficulty. But at the same time I know that I can only manage a few mountain walks! There is in me an aspiration which I must translate realistically into what I am actually capable of doing. The same applies to the figure of David, who can be described as an authentic man, a real man, who knows the gifts which the Lord has given him and whose ambitions do not exceed his abilities. Often we are thoroughly discontented because we should like to do everything and have everything, and since we cannot, we do not even aim for the little achievements which are within our grasp.

> *"Grant, O Lord, that I may know myself and that I may value the real gifts which you have given me, without deluding myself with false ambitions."*

Authenticity is difficult at any stage of our existence, especially for those who occupy positions of responsibility. People say to me, "You are the Bishop and of course you must know this, you must be able to tell us about this, that or the other thing as well!" How am I to explain that being a bishop does not mean that I am able to talk on any subject? How am I to explain that the Bishop is still a man with limitations like so many others?

There is, therefore, in us, either actively (where we are concerned) or passively (where others are concerned) what amounts to a habit of inflating reality, to turn ourselves to "personalities" or turn others into "personalities", departing from the truth of the Gospel and from the simplicity of relationships. We must continually learn to enjoy the gifts we have without becoming arrogant, and not to be downcast by those which we do not possess and which others do. This equilibrium is exactly the opposite to what we have seen in the epileptic boy: his habit of throwing himself to the ground and grinding his teeth are actions typical of someone who, wanting to do more than he can, ends up by doing much less than he could.

The strength of the Lord

We can fully grasp what is meant by *the strength of the Lord* if we continue reading the passage after David has taken off Saul's armour. These are verses I Samuel 17:40-51:

> "He took his stick in his hand, selected five smooth stones from the river bed and put them in his shepherd's bag, in his pouch; then, sling in hand, he walked towards the Philistine. The Philistine, preceded by his shield-bearer, came nearer and nearer to David. When the Philistine looked David up and down, what he saw filled

him with scorn, because David was only a lad, with ruddy cheeks and an attractive appearance. The Philistine said to David, 'Am I a dog for you to come after me with sticks?' And the Philistine cursed David by his gods.

The Philistine said to David, 'Come over here and I will give your flesh to the birds of the air and the wild beasts!' David retorted to the Philistine, 'You come to me with sword, spear and scimitar, but I come to you in the name of Yahweh Sabaoth, God of the armies of Israel, whom you have challenged. Today, Yahweh will deliver you into my hand; I shall kill you, I shall cut off your head; today, I shall give your corpse and the corpses of the Philistine army to the birds of the air and the wild beasts, so that the whole world may know that there is a God in Israel, and this whole assembly know that Yahweh does not give victory by means of sword and spear – for Yahweh is lord of the battle and he will deliver you into our power.'

No sooner had the Philistine started forward to confront David than David darted out of the lines and ran to meet the Philistine. Putting his hand in his bag, he took out a stone, slung it and struck the Philistine on the forehead; the stone penetrated his forehead and he fell face downwards on the ground. Thus David triumphed over the Philistine with a sling and a stone; he hit the Philistine and killed him, though he had no sword in his hand. David ran and stood over the Philistine, seized his sword, pulled it from the scabbard, despatched him and cut off his head."

David has taken hold of his staff, chosen five smooth stones from the stream and placed them in his shepherd's bag. He grasps the sling and goes towards the Philistine. David's maturity is summed up by his answer, which is a masterpiece of Biblical faith: "I come to you in the name of Yahweh Sabaoth, God of the armies of Israel…"

At what age is this strength given? The real question, however, is this: "At what age can the clear-sightedness be granted to go and fight a difficult battle *in the strength of the Lord?".* My answer is: "At any age". A calling can therefore be very serious at any age *if* it is founded on this knowledge of oneself and of God. If that person knows their own limitations, their own desires and also has knowledge of the strength of the Lord, then in such a case, it is serious enough to overcome any enemy.

> *I can say in all sincerity that the clarity of my vocation came to me when I was ten or eleven. I still well remember the circumstances of prayer and meditation and I feel that the definitive choice I made then remains the same today.*

I can say in all sincerity that the clarity of my vocation (that is of the *Who am I?* and *Who is God for me?* and therefore of my readiness to entrust myself to God) came to me when I was ten or eleven. I still well remember the circumstances of prayer and meditation and I feel that the definitive choice I made then remains the same today. Naturally, my commitment has now strengthened, it has overcome some difficulties and yet it is substantially the same. If anyone should ask me whether my vocation was serious when I was ten or eleven, my answer would have to be: "It was so serious that I believe that today it is the same vocation and that it has undergone no substantial change."

Nevertheless, even here we must not aspire to more than God gives us. If God gives me the certainty now, I will try to follow with humility. It is for us to say: "Lord, I come in your strength!" Peter answered Jesus in the same way when he said he would pay out the fishing net. It is the assent of Mary: "You see before you the Lord's servant, let it happen to me as you have said." It is we who must answer because the Lord leaves us free and does not answer for us.

If we have not then yet reached a certain measure of clarity we can seek help in order to progress towards this. We need to pray so that each of us can welcome God's plan as and when it is given to us.

You have given me victory, O Lord

I shall leave you to study the third point of our meditation on your own. Read psalm 18; re-read it slowly, thinking about everything we have said about David and about his way of facing the fight. Try to make the words of the psalmist your own, with the desire of growing in readiness for God's call and in trusting surrender to God's word and to his plan for each one of you and for your lives.

Psalm 18 – A King's Thanksgiving

I love you, Yahweh, my strength
(my Saviour, you have saved me from violence).

Yahweh is my rock and my fortress,
my deliverer is my God.
I take refuge in him, my rock,
my shield, my saving strength,
my stronghold, my place of refuge.

I call to Yahweh who is worthy of praise,
and I am saved from my foes.

With Death's breakers closing in on me,
Belial's torrents ready to swallow me,
Sheol's snares every side of me,
Death's traps lying ahead of me.

I called to Yahweh in my anguish,
I cried for help to my God;
from his Temple he heard my voice,
my cry came to his ears.

Then the earth quaked and rocked,
the mountains' foundations shuddered,
they quaked at his blazing anger,
Smoke rose from his nostrils,
from his mouth devouring fire
(coals were kindled at it).

He parted the heavens and came down,
a storm-cloud beneath his feet;
riding one of the winged creatures, he flew,
soaring on the wings of the wind.

His covering he made the darkness,
his pavilion dark waters and dense cloud.
A brightness lit up before him,
hail and blazing fire.

Yahweh thundered from the heavens,
the Most High made his voice heard.
He shot his arrows and scattered them,
he hurled his lightning and routed them.

The very springs of ocean were exposed,
the world's foundations were laid bare,
at your roaring, Yahweh,
at the blast of breath from your nostrils!

He reached down from on high, snatched me up,
pulled me from the watery depths,
rescued me from the mighty foe,
from my enemies who were stronger than I.

They assailed me on my day of disaster
but Yahweh was there to support me;
he freed me, set me at large,
he rescued me because he loves me.

Yahweh rewards me for my uprightness,
as my hands are pure, so he repays me,
since I have kept the ways of Yahweh,
and not fallen away from my God.

His judgements are all before me,
his statutes I have not put away from me.
I am blameless before him,
I keep myself clear of evil.

So Yahweh repaid me for acting uprightly
because he could see I was pure.
You are faithful to the faithful,
blameless with the blameless,

sincere to the sincere,
but cunning to the crafty,
you save a people that is humble
and humiliate those with haughty looks.

Yahweh, you yourself are my lamp,
my God lights up my darkness;
with you I storm the rampart,
with my God I can scale any wall.

This God, his way is blameless;
the word of Yahweh is refined in the furnace,
for he alone is the shield
of all who take refuge in him.

For who is God but Yahweh,
who is a rock but our God?
This God who girds me with strength,
who makes my way free from blame,

who makes me as swift as a deer
and sets me firmly on the heights,
who trains my hands for battle,
my arms to bend a bow of bronze.

You give me your invincible shield
(your right hand upholds me)
you never cease to listen to me,
you give me the strides of a giant,
give me ankles that never weaken.

I pursue my enemies and overtake them,
not turning back till they are annihilated;

I strike them down and they cannot rise,
they fall, they are under my feet.

You have girded me with strength for the fight,
bent down my assailants beneath me,
made my enemies retreat before me;
and those who hate me I destroy.

They cry out, there is no one to save;
to Yahweh, but no answer comes.
I crumble them like dust before the wind,
trample them like the mud of the streets.

You free me from the quarrels of my people,
you place me at the head of the nations,
a people I did not know are now my servants;

foreigners came wooing my favour,
no sooner do they hear than they obey me;
foreigners grow faint of heart,
they come trembling out of their fastnesses.

Life to Yahweh! Blessed be my rock!
Exalted be the God of my salvation,
the God who gives me vengeance,
and subjects whole peoples to me,

who rescues me from my raging enemies.
You lift me high above those who attack me,
you deliver me from the man of violence.

For this I will praise you, Yahweh, among the nations,
and sing praise to your name.

He saves his king time after time,
displays his faithful love for his anointed,
for David and his heirs for ever.

The fifth dialogue
The ability to repent
David and the trap

As literature, the books of the Old Testament differ greatly from each other. Some are direct and simple; others are complex and poetic. The Book of Job, for example, is highly poetic, very difficult to translate and hard to understand. Then there are the narrative masterpieces, among the best pages of which are those telling the story of Joseph and the story of David.

The story of David is rich in humanity, pathos and humour; it also contains unparalleled wisdom. The description of David's transgression is among the most fascinating and humanly true. We find this story in the Second Book of Samuel in chapter 11, and in chapter 12 where the drama comes to an end; it can be of great help to us in understanding who we are, who I am. The events are narrated not just to tell us who David was but to teach us *who humankind is*, who I am, and then to teach us who God is.

I should like to re-live this biblical episode with you, making myself re-live it in the first person, as if staging a re-enactment. I imagine that I am David and, at this point in my life, I place myself in his situation, and I ask myself *Who am I, David?* I can reply immediately: *I am a person whom God has called, to whom God has willed great good*, because when I was a goatherd no-one knew me. At a certain point, God took me, gave me great strength and made me accomplish an act of courage against Goliath. I did not shrink from doing this and so God took hold of me with even greater strength and made me one of the greatest kings in the history of my people. I must therefore thank God for choosing me in my poverty and multiplying my powers:

> *I praise you and I thank you, my God; I love you because you are my strength, because you have given me a just heart. I have never profited from my strength at the expense of my enemies, nor against those who betrayed me; I have also been merciful to people. Lord, you have made me good and have given me a great spirit of prayer. For thousands of years all nations will pray with the prayers which you, my God, have placed upon my lips.*

David is a man who acknowledges that he has received great gifts from God; that he was chosen and that he responded; that he is capable of true prayer. Many of the psalms were composed, or at least inspired, by him. I will choose one at random:

> "My heart is ready, God,
> I will sing and make music;
> Come, my glory!
> Awake, lyre and harp,
> I will awake the Dawn!
> I will praise you among the peoples, Yahweh…"
> (Psalm 108:1–3)

The Lord has made David a good, just, prudent man, strong in war and modest in victory, who is not corrupt. And yet, at a certain point, even for David danger awaits.

David in the trap (II Samuel 11)

The self-deception into which David falls is like a trap which can snap shut on any one of us if we are not vigilant. How does David begin to walk into the trap?

> *Here we already have the first trap: so far David has lived his life with great energy and increasingly wishes to rest on his laurels; he is falling prey to vanity.*

a) "At the turn of the year, at the time when kings go campaigning, David sent Joab and with him his guards…They massacred the Ammonites…David, however, remained in Jerusalem" (II Samuel 11:1). He must have thought: "*Now I have already achieved a great deal!*" Here we already have the first trap: so far David has lived his life with great energy and increasingly wishes to rest on his laurels; he is falling prey to vanity.

While he was at home, "towards evening when David had got up from resting and was strolling on the palace roof…he saw a woman bathing; the woman was very beautiful" (v. 2). He thinks he is now a mature man and that he can therefore look at anything, in the certainty that he can control his feelings. He imagines that he stands absolutely no chance of being disturbed by a little voyeurism. Being so sure of himself, and saying "This is really nothing to me," marks the beginning of a *confusion in his feelings*, which takes hold of him, gnaws away at him and causes him to take the second downward step.

b) "David made enquiries about this woman and was told, 'Why, that is Bathsheba daughter of Eliam and wife of Uriah the Hittite.'" (v. 3). David deludes himself that there can be no harm in knowing who she is, that this will not change anything; and then it occurs to him that Uriah, the woman's husband, is far away. "David then sent messengers to fetch her. She came to him, and he lay with her, just after she had purified herself from her period. She then went home again." (v. 4).

> *We have come to the second stage.*
> *David knows he should not do*
> *what he wants to do but thinks that*
> *no-one will find out and that will*
> *be the end of it.*

We have come to the second stage. David knows he should not do what he wants to do but *thinks that no-one will find out and that will be the end of it.* Yes, it's certainly a moment of weakness but he is convinced that he will think no more about it.

c) But David, without realising it, steps down to *the third step*. "The woman conceived and sent word to David, 'I am pregnant'" (v. 5). David unexpectedly finds himself faced by a situation he has not foreseen. He who was so astute, who could keep everything under control, has now begun to know fear, because he is no longer sure what to do. Then, however, he thinks: "*I'm clever and, despite everything, I shall manage to get away with it this time!*"

"David then sent word to Joab, 'Send me Uriah the Hittite,' whereupon Joab sent Uriah to David. When Uriah reached him, David asked how Joab was and how the army was and how the war was going. David then said to Uriah, 'Go down to your house and wash your feet,'" (vv. 6–8). David seems very calm because he was a great diplomat: he finds out how the war is going and then suggests Uriah should get a bit of rest, that he should go home to eat, drink, sleep and be with his wife.

d) "Uriah, however, slept at the palace gate with all his master's bodyguard" (v. 9). David thought that with his cunning he would be able to sort everything out and instead he is trapped. He is trapped by his feelings because he realises that he loves the woman and then because he sees and he is beginning to think fondly of the baby which will be born to her.

> *He is trapped because the only way out he could have taken was to confess his sin, but he did not dare to do this.*

He is trapped by his feelings because he likes Uriah, who is one of his faithful soldiers, and he is ashamed to have done him wrong, to have betrayed him. He is trapped because the only way out he could have taken was to confess his sin, but he did not dare to do this. Perhaps it seems to him that a king cannot admit that he has made such a mess of things: he would have lost a great deal of his dignity!

> *This man who had always been good, mild, prudent and wise, no longer knows which way to turn. Night and day, he is tormented by his dilemma: "What shall I do?*

This man who had always been good, mild, prudent and wise, no longer knows which way to turn. Night and day, he is tormented by his dilemma: "What shall I do? What should I sacrifice? My reputation? No! The woman? Again, no, I don't want to! The child? Not that either. My friend? No! And no matter what I do, in the end I'm the one who'll be to blame for everything."

David began by giving in a bit, to a bit of curiosity: he has always taken pleasure in his ability to fix things, and now he is up against it. The Biblical text tells how David summons Uriah a second time, gets him drunk, tries to befuddle him in order to make him go home to his wife, but Uriah, who has perhaps sensed that something is up, remains unmoved and decides not to go home.

We can pause here for a moment's reflection: *what has happened to David?* He has experienced his own frailty. If someone had told him a month, or even a week earlier, that he was about to turn into an unjust, adulterous man, that he was going to run the risk of killing his best friend, he would certainly have replied: *"No, I would never behave like that!"*. Now, however, David is desperate, and, consumed by rage, he thinks of a way of escaping this mess.

e) The next morning he writes a letter to Joab and makes Uriah deliver it to him personally; it contains his order that Uriah be put in the front line so that he will be killed.

The story becomes dramatic and brutal: Uriah dies in front of the city walls. When the news reaches David, the king pretends to fly into a rage, to weep for the death of his friend. He has entered into a state of such shameful pretence that he is no longer even aware of it. If we could make David talk, he would say to us: "Yes, I believed I was a man of integrity: honest, just and true; instead there came a point when I felt so full of falseness that I was ashamed of myself. I simulated feelings which I did not feel, I pretended to weep when I was, in fact, glad that Uriah, my friend, was dead. I pretended to be angry about my army's defeat whereas this was what I wanted."

> *David is the image of the man who, despite having the best intentions, the most noble premises, the most scrupulous upbringing, is, and remains, frail and weak.*

David is the image of the man who, despite having the best intentions, the most noble premises, the most scrupulous upbringing, is, and remains, frail and weak. Had he said at once: "I have made a mistake, I have been imprudent, I must draw back," he would have interrupted the spiral of death. But time after time, he convinced himself that he could cope, that he was astute enough to put things right and in doing so arrived at the utmost degradation.

> *Understanding who man is, who I am, means understanding the plea: "Lord, without your hand on my head, I am a poor, frail, weak sinner."*

When I start to lose my belief in this truth, to rely on myself, to fail to acknowledge my small faults, to gamble with my feelings, I run the risk of being trapped and falling into one snare after another, ending up by finding myself where I should never have been.

> If we read some verses from the Gospel according to Mark, we can pray: "Lord, you have spoken about the heart of a man and you said: 'For it is from within, from the heart, that evil intentions emerge: fornication, theft, murder, adultery, avarice, malice, deceit, indecency, envy, slander, pride, folly. All these evil things come from within and make a person unclean.'" (Mark 7:21–23)
>
> Lord, grant that I may understand that the roots of these things exist in my heart. If I really want to know who I am, I must understand the greatness and strength of my calling – and also that well of darkness and frailty which is inside me. For until I acknowledge this, my personality will not be completely free; I will fail to achieve the integrity and truthfulness in my actions possessed by those who acknowledge that they are weak and continually turn to you as their Saviour."

"I have sinned against you" (II Samuel 12)

How does David get out of the trap? We are told how in chapter 12 in the Second Book of Samuel. The prophet Nathan goes to see David, who receives him. Nathan informs him of a situation involving two men, one rich, one poor. The rich man had many flocks and herds, the poor man only one little ewe lamb. The rich man, having need of some meat to serve in his own house, took the poor man's lamb, thus depriving him of what little he had. At this point in the prophet's story, David could not contain his anger and he said to Nathan: 'As Yahweh lives…the man who did this deserves to die! For doing such a thing and for having shown no pity, he shall make fourfold restitution for the lamb.' (II Samuel 12:5–6)

Note that David, even if he is overreacting (the theft committed by the rich man cannot be compared with the death which David has plotted), shows that he has a deep sense of justice. Although he is going through a very damaging experience, he still knows the meaning of truth. He is, however, unable to apply it to his own situation: he criticises others, accuses them, judges them, while the self-deception to which he has fallen prey prevents him from seeing his own sin.

At this point, the prophet exclaims: 'You are the man! Yahweh, God of Israel, says this, "I anointed you king of Israel, I saved you from Saul's clutches, I gave you your master's household and your master's wives into your arms, I gave you the House of Israel and the House of Judah…Why did you show contempt for Yahweh, by doing what displeases him?"' (vv. 7–9). Now David recovers his clear-sightedness and he confesses: 'I have sinned against Yahweh' (v. 13). These are the words which could have saved him at the outset and it is only now that he manages to say them, having ruined himself, his reputation and his conscience.

Traps which lie in wait for us

I suggest you read the story carefully once more and take note of all its subtleties and fine detail because it is full of very accurate psychological insights.

What does our enemy want of us? Our enemy wants to confound us.
Even without reaching such excesses (David represents a pathological case), each time we give in to some temptation, the enemy sees to it that it is followed by another. Confusion mounts: weary of ourselves, discouraged, scared, we tell ourselves that we cannot cope, that we shall never be able to manage. An omission, a flash of bad temper, a failure, as well as a sin, can become the point of departure from which we start to head for the trap which our enemy prepares.

The truth of our being, however, is reawakened every time that we say: "I have sinned, I have made a mistake," every time that we acknowledge that we have proved vulnerable to some form of laziness, to a moment of frailty.

> *"O Lord, teach us to fight day by day, to struggle for our truth and our integrity. Teach us, through the miraculous gift of the Sacrament of Reconciliation, to tell the truth about ourselves and to find the joy of this truth."*

The Sacrament of Penance or Reconciliation is one of the fundamental means of restoring the truthfulness of a person, when we reach the point where we can tell everything about ourselves, express ourselves, regain our balance and invoke the power of the Lord's forgiveness for ourselves.

> *"Grant, O Lord, that we may not neglect the gift of Penitence which you have placed in our hands. And grant us the ability to grasp those small realities, apparently of little importance, but which can nevertheless trigger emotional disturbance and insecurity in our lives."*

Anything that makes us disturbed, tired, bored, melancholy, has its causes which will be identified and brought to light: the Lord is light, the Lord is joy: the Lord wants us to be truthful and joyful.

Pray Psalm 51

Psalm 51 expresses all the force of truth which David experienced in that moment when he found the courage to look into his heart and to see clearly for himself the negative experience he has been through. It is one of the most beautiful psalms and I suggest you read it as a prayer and then meditate on it, asking yourselves: "What is there of David in me, in that moment in which he responds to the words of the Prophet, and what is revealed by the expressions of this Psalm?" You can underline the verse which says the most to you, which you feel is most relevant to your situation.

> *"Lord, help us to read this psalm while thinking of our own faults, both large and small, because every sin, even the one which seems trifling, has introduced a harmful process into our lives which could be like that of David."*

Scripture Texts
David's transgression

Second Book of Samuel: Chapter 11:1–25

> At the turn of the year, at the time when kings go campaigning, David sent Joab and with him his guards and all Israel. They massacred the Ammonites and laid siege to Rabbah-of-the-Ammonites. David, however, remained in Jerusalem.

It happened towards evening when David had got up from resting and was strolling on the palace roof, that from the roof he saw a woman bathing; the woman was very beautiful. David made enquiries about this woman and was told, 'Why, that is Bathsheba daughter of Eliam and wife of Uriah the Hittite.' David then sent messengers to fetch her. She came to him, and he lay with her, just after she had purified herself from her period. She then went home again. The woman conceived and sent word to David, 'I am pregnant.'

David then sent word to Joab, 'Send me Uriah the Hittite,' whereupon Joab sent Uriah to David. When Uriah reached him, David asked how Joab was and how the army was and how the war was going. David then said to Uriah, 'Go down to your house and wash your feet.' Uriah left the palace and was followed by a present from the king's table. Uriah, however, slept at the palace gate with all his master's bodyguard and did not go down to his house.

This was reported to David; 'Uriah', the said 'has not gone down to his house.' So David asked Uriah, 'Haven't you just arrived from the journey? Why didn't you go down to your house?' To which Uriah replied, 'The ark, Israel and Judah are lodged in huts; my master Joab and my lord's guards are camping in the open. Am I to go to my house, then, and eat and drink and sleep with my wife? As Yahweh lives, and as you yourself live, I shall do no such thing!' David then said to Uriah, 'Stay on here today; tomorrow I shall send you off.' So Uriah stayed that day in Jerusalem. The next day, David invited him to eat and drink in his presence and made him drunk. In the evening, Uriah went out and bedded down with his master's bodyguard, bud did not go down to his house.

Next morning David wrote a letter to Joab and sent it by Uriah. In the letter he wrote, 'Put Uriah out in front where the fighting is fiercest and then fall back, so that he gets wounded and killed.' Joab, then besieging the city, stationed Uriah at a point where he knew that there would be tough fighters. The people of the city sallied out and engaged Joab; there were casualties in the army, among David's guards, and Uriah the Hittite was killed as well.

Joab sent David a full account of the battle. To the messenger he gave his order: 'When you have finished telling the king all about the battle, if the king's anger is aroused and he says, "Why did you go near the town to give battle? Didn't you know that they would shoot from the ramparts? Who killed Abimelech son of Jerubbaal? Wasn't it a woman who dropped a millstone on him from the ramparts, causing his death at Thebez? Why did you go near the ramparts?" you are to say, "Your servant Uriah the Hittite is dead too." '

So the messenger set off and, on his arrival, told David everything that Joab had instructed him to say. David flew into a rage with Joab and said to the messenger, 'Why did you go near the ramparts? Who killed Abimelech son of Jerubbaal? Wasn't it a woman who dropped a millstone on him from the ramparts, causing his death at Thebez? Why did you go near the ramparts?' The messenger replied to David, 'Their men had won an initial advantage and then came out to engage us in the open. We then drove them back into the gateway, but the archers shot at your retainers from the ramparts; some of the king's retainers lost their lives, and your servant Uriah the Hittite is dead too.'

David then said to the messenger, 'Say this to Joab, "Do not take the matter to heart; the sword devours now one and now another. Attack the town in greater force and destroy it." That will encourage him.'

Yahweh sent the prophet Nathan to David. He came to him and said: In the same town were two men, one rich, the other poor. The rich man had flocks and herds in great abundance; the poor man had nothing but a ewe lamb, only a single little one which he had bought. He fostered it and it grew up with him and his children, eating his bread, drinking from his cup, sleeping in his arms; it was like a daughter to him. When a traveller came to stay, the rich man would not take anything from his own flock or herd to provide for the wayfarer who had come to him. Instead, he stole the poor man's lamb and prepared that for his guest.

David flew into a great rage with the man. 'As Yahweh lives,' he said to Nathan 'the man who did this deserves to die. For doing such a thing and for having shown no pity, he shall make fourfold restitution for the lamb.'

Nathan then said to David, 'You are the man! Yahweh, God of Israel, says this, "I anointed you king of Israel, I saved you from Saul's clutches, I gave you your master's household and your master's wives into your arms, I gave you the House of Israel and the House of Judah; and, if this is still too little, I shall give you other things as well. Why did you show contempt for Yahweh, by doing what displeases him? You put Uriah the Hittite to the sword, you took his wife to be your wife, causing his death by the sword of the Ammonites. For this, your household will never be free of the sword, since you showed contempt for me and took the wife of Uriah the Hittite, to make her your wife."

'Yahweh says this, "Out of your own household I shall raise misfortune for you. Before your very eyes I shall take your wives and give them to your neighbour, who will lie with your wives in broad daylight. You have worked in secret, but I shall work this for all Israel to see, in broad daylight".'

David said to Nathan, 'I have sinned against Yahweh.' Nathan then said to David, 'Yahweh, for his part , forgives your sin; you are not to die. But, since you have outraged Yahweh by doing this, the child born to you will die.'

David's repentance
Psalm 51

Have mercy on me, O God, in your faithful love,
in your great tenderness wipe away my offences;
wash me thoroughly from my guilt,
purify me from my sin.

For I am well aware of my offences,
my sin is constantly in mind.
Against you, you alone, I have sinned,
I have done what you see to be wrong,

That you may show your saving justice when you pass sentence,
and your victory may appear when you give judgement,
remember I was born guilty,
a sinner from the moment of my conception.

But you delight in sincerity of heart,
and in secret you teach me wisdom.
Purify me with hyssop till I am clean,
wash me till I am whiter than snow.

Let me hear the sound of joy and gladness,
and the bones you have crushed will dance.
Turn away your face from my sins,
and wipe away all my guilt.

God, create in me a clean heart,
renew within me a resolute spirit,
do not thrust me away from your presence,
do not take away from me your spirit of holiness.

Give me back the joy of your salvation,
sustain in me a generous spirit.
I shall teach the wicked your paths,
and sinners will return to you.

Deliver me from bloodshed, God, God of my salvation,
and my tongue will acclaim your saving justice.
Lord, open my lips,
and my mouth will speak out your praise.

Sacrifice gives you no pleasure,
burnt offering you do not desire.
Sacrifice to God is a broken spirit,
a broken, contrite heart you never scorn.

In your graciousness do good to Zion,
rebuild the walls of Jerusalem.
Then you will delight in upright sacrifices,
–burnt offerings and whole oblations–
and young bulls will be offered on your altar.

Psalm 108

My heart is ready, God
I will sing and make music;
come, my glory!
Awake, lyre and harp,
I will awake the Dawn!

I will praise you among the peoples, Yahweh,
I will play to you among the nations,
for your faithful love towers to heaven,
and your constancy to the clouds.

Be exalted above the heavens, God.
Your glory over the whole earth!

To rescue those you love,
save with your right hand and answer us.

God has spoken from his sanctuary,
'In triumph I will divide up Shechem,
and share out the valley of Succoth.

'Mine is Gilead, mine Manasseh,
Ephraim the helmet on my head,
Judah my commander's baton,

Moab a bowl for me to wash in,
on Edom I will plant my sandal,
over Philistia I cry victory.'

Who will lead me against a fortified city,
who will guide me into Edom,
if not you, the God who has rejected us?
God, you who no longer march with our armies.

Bring us help in our time of crisis,
any human assistance is worthless.
With God we shall do deeds of valour,
he will trample down our enemies.

The sixth dialogue
How to meet the Lord

How to meet the Lord

The following readings are a response to the wish which many of you have expressed to me, verbally or in writing: how can we learn to pray better, to make closer contact with the Lord?

The readings indicate two special moments when we meet God. The first, suggested by the reading from Matthew's gospel, is in *contemplation*. The second, suggested by the reading from Genesis, is through *being tested*.

First Reading: Genesis 28:10–19

"Jacob left Beersheba and set out for Haran. When he had reached a certain place, he stopped there for the night, since the sun had set. Taking one of the stones of that place, he made it his pillow and lay down where he was. He had a dream: there was a ladder, planted on the ground with its top reaching to heaven; and God's angels were going up and down on it. And there was Yahweh, standing beside him and saying, 'I, Yahweh, am the God of Abraham your father, and the God of Isaac. The ground on which you are lying I shall give to you and your descendants. Your descendants will be as plentiful as the dust on the ground; you will spread out to west and east, to north and south, and all clans on earth will bless themselves by you and your descendants. Be sure, I am with you; I shall keep you safe wherever you go, and bring you back to this country, for I shall never desert you until I have done what I have promised you.

Then Jacob awoke from his sleep and said, 'Truly, Yahweh is in this place and I did not know!' He was afraid and said, 'How awe-inspiring this place is! This is nothing less than the abode of God, and this is the gate of heaven!' Early next morning, Jacob took the stone he had used for his pillow, and set it up as a pillar, pouring oil over the top of it. He named the place Bethel, but before that the town had been called Luz."

Second Reading: Proverbs 3:19–26

"In wisdom, Yahweh laid the earth's foundations,
in understanding, he spread out the heavens.
Through his knowledge the depths were cleft open,
and the clouds distil the dew.

My child, hold to sound advice and prudence,
never let them out of sight;
they will give life to your soul
and beauty to your neck.
You will go on your way in safety,
your feet will not stumble.
When you go to bed, you will not be afraid,
having gone to bed, your sleep will be sweet.
Have not fear either of sudden terror
or of attack mounted by wicked men,
since Yahweh will be your guarantor,
he will keep your steps from the snare."

Gospel Reading: Matthew 6:1–6

" 'Be careful not to parade your uprightness in public to attract attention; otherwise you will lose all reward from your Father in heaven. So when you give alms, do not have it trumpeted before you; this is what the hypocrites do in the synagogues and in the streets to win human admiration. In truth I tell you, they have had their reward. But when you give alms, your left hand must not know what your right is doing; your almsgiving must be secret, and your Father who is in that secret place, and your Father who sees all that is done in secret will reward you.

'And when you pray, do not imitate the hypocrites: they love to say their prayers standing up in the synagogues and at the street corners for people to see them. In truth I tell you, they have had their reward. But when you pray, go to your private room, shut yourself in, and so pray to your Father who is in that secret place, and your Father who sees all that is done in secret will reward you'."

The secret of contemplation

When you want to meet God, 'go to your private room, shut yourself in, and so pray to your Father who is in that secret place, and your Father who sees all that is done in secret will reward you.' Jesus, with these very simple words, teaches us a method – the secret of contemplation. Often we need a certain atmosphere in order to spend some time in true prayer. We have to withdraw into our own room, detach ourselves, and not talk with other people or listen to anything: we have to collect ourselves. This has a deep psychological meaning because it underlines the fact that our strengths are often dissipated. When we talk, listen, laugh, move about, we are distracted in a thousand ways.

In order to meet God, we have to draw our energies back within ourselves and concentrate, we have to remove ourselves, in a manner of speaking, from the external world. The meaning of the word concentration is in fact to have a single centre: if we place ourselves before the Lord in this way, amazing gifts are freed within us. We even appear different to ourselves, gaining a lucidity and clear-sightedness we have never known before, and we can better understand the question *Who am I?*

Eastern spirituality – even outside the Christian tradition – has had much to say on the theme of contemplation. The image eastern traditions usually employ to express contemplation is that of the tiger or panther, which before launching itself in an attack on its prey, gathers itself together to gain maximum strength.

During the time of retreat it is fairly normal for us to experience this meeting with God in contemplation, but of course we need to continue with it afterwards. I often find myself distracted by visits, audiences, telephone calls, news: but when I do finally manage to gather my thoughts together, I see more clearly what God wants of me, what I should do, what is really important. And then my strength is renewed.

There is a secret to contemplation! I have had the opportunity of seeing that the Pope has known it and lived it daily. During the very taxing journeys which he undertakes, when he has to talk continuously, he always manages to find some time, even if it is only a few minutes, in which he can collect his thoughts in silence. At such times he appears to detach himself from everything and everyone because he remains immobile, concentrated. I happened to notice this when we were both in a helicopter. First thing in the morning, before starting a busy and stressful day, he withdrew into himself in absolute silence and stillness. I believe that it is because of his profound spirituality that he is so full of strength when he speaks.

> *A second special moment in which to meet the Lord is at times of unhappiness.*

The secret of being tested

A second special moment in which to meet the Lord is at times of unhappiness. The reading from Genesis shows how Jacob lived through just such a moment. Forced to flee from his home, he finds himself alone, not knowing whether anyone will help him or even what his future might be. His anguish and solitude oppress him and he experiences deep unhappiness.

All of a sudden, however, he senses that God is with him and he hears the word: 'I, Yahweh, am the God of Abraham, your father, and the God of Isaac. The ground on which you are lying I shall give to you and your descendants...Be sure, I am with you; I shall keep you safe wherever you go...'

All this happens because Jacob understands the secret of being put to the test, and he is able to live through his difficult moment before God. Usually, when we find ourselves in difficulty, we complain, we moan and protest. If, instead of doing this, we can manage to gather our thoughts together and say: "Lord, why are you allowing this to happen? What do you want of me? What do you mean to do with my life? What is your word for me?", then our horizon would clear and we would feel that God is with us even when we are being tested.

> *"Who, Lord, are you?". "I am the one who will never abandon you. I shall keep you safe wherever you go."*

"Who, Lord, are you?". "I am the one who will never abandon you. I shall keep you safe wherever you go." The impact of these words addressed to us, to me, vanquish all fear. No road is now too difficult to travel, there is no more loneliness, no physical or mental suffering that cannot be overcome; and we learn to pray, we find the Lord, we see the path we must take.

Mary's experience

This is how Mary, the mother of Jesus, came to know God. During the most private state of contemplation – at the time of the Annunciation; and during her terrible time of trial – at the time of the Crucifixion of Jesus. In silence and suffering Mary knew God in a way in which not one of us can ever know him!

If we turn to Mary, she will certainly teach us in what ways the Lord wants to meet us.

"Lord, I thank you for these moments of contemplation which you give us. I also thank you, although in a rather fearful voice, for those testing times during which I experience your presence here with me. And you, Mary, bestow upon us the gift of strength, the experience of prayer and of the knowledge of God in contemplation and in times of trial. In this way, through us, God will make himself known to other sisters and brothers and we will be able to become his witnesses. Jesus, you who are about to come among us, beside us, within us during the Eucharist, help us to grow in the true knowledge of the Father until we know him as you know him!"

The seventh dialogue
Paul

Help us!

In this meditation I would like to ponder more deeply the question *Who, Lord, are you?* And I would like to ponder it more deeply by sharing with you what I have discovered during our days together, while I was reflecting on a passage from the Acts of the Apostles. The passage in question is one which I have read and meditated upon many times and yet I had never thought about it in the context of the question *Who, Lord, are you?*

First of all, we can read the passage together, from Acts 16.

> "They travelled through Phrygia and the Galatian country, because they had been told by the Holy Spirit not to preach the word in Asia. When they reached the frontier of Mysia they tried to go into Bithynia, but as the Spirit of Jesus would not allow them, they went through Mysia and came down to Troas.
>
> One night Paul had a vision: a Macedonian appeared and kept urging him in these words, 'Come across to Macedonia and help us.' Once he had seen this vision we lost no time in arranging a passage to Macedonia, convinced that God had called us to bring them the good news."
> *Acts 16:6–10*

Let us try to select three aspects of the story:
1. the first is Paul's *frustration*;
2. the second is Paul's euphoria, or rather, *Paul at the cultural turning point;*
3. the third is *the new calling*.

Paul's frustration

The first two verses of this passage convey the sense of frustration and monotony which Paul is experiencing. The apostle would like to preach in a certain place but this is not possible; he is also prevented from doing so elsewhere. By this means the Spirit of the Lord has let it be understood that what Paul has in mind is not what needs to be done. He is therefore forced to live his daily life without those opportunities which his zealous spirit demands.

> *Monotony makes itself felt not only as a burden but also as a temptation, making us do things out of sheer habit.*

We can assume that he is experiencing monotony – days pass which are all alike. I must say that it is through experiences of yours, which you have shared with me, that I have come to understand the experience of Paul: "You help us to overcome the burden of everyday monotony… We have a good beginning to the school year but after a few months we are tired of the activities and timetables which are always identical…" Monotony makes itself felt not only as a burden but also as a temptation, making us do things out of sheer habit.

Now we see that Paul is undergoing this very same test because his scope for action is limited and restricted by circumstances. When it comes down to it, what is daily monotony other than the limitation of our actions by timetables, by the environment of the seminary or workplace, by the subjects being studied, by the usual rhythm of life? This is a real state of mind and we are right to face it.

When I think of my years at the seminary or as a student, I remember very clearly indeed that I went through periods during which monotony really oppressed me; there was a routine for my life, at least in the ordinary course of events, from which we departed occasionally for an excursion or for some special event.

So what should we do? I believe that we should enlarge our horizons a little, trying to cope with the difficulties we are going through in a rational way. We may then discover that the burden of everyday life weighs upon so many other people as well. I'm thinking of the letters that I receive from mothers, from men, from young people, and which bear witness to the stress of everyday life. The experience of work brings with it a certain satisfaction, it is true, and yet it is confined to certain duties, limited in various ways: one can sense the strain of having to persevere. As a boy I used to fantasise sometimes, wanting to break this monotony, and I used to say to myself: "When I grow up, I will be a journalist and then I'll be able to travel a lot, get to know new places all the time, find myself in situations that are always different." Nowadays, I meet a great many journalists who tell me in confidence: "My everyday life is so monotonous! It looks attractive but in reality it is restricted by the newspaper!"

> *We have to accept our condition and feel that it unites us with others, with the overwhelming majority of men and women.*

Each one of us, therefore, within his or her own environment, has to face the same situations day after day. It's difficult to escape from this burden. Actors, atheletes, politicians – all the people whom perhaps we envy cannot escape from it. We have to accept our condition and feel that it unites us with others, with the overwhelming majority of men and women. By living my everyday monotony I become part of the life of the whole of humanity. And to this life of the whole of humanity, I bring my moment of grace, of sacrifice, of commitment, of renunciation, so that a great many people can have the courage to begin again and to live.

Paul, in his frustration and in his apparently enforced immobility, provides us with a worthwhile lesson.

Paul at the cultural turning point

I mentioned *Paul's moment of euphoria*. I infer this from our passage by reading it in the light of a personal memory. At verse 8 we read that Paul and his followers, having attempted to travel through various regions and having been repeatedly turned back onto the same road, "went through Misia and came down to Troas."

Troas is a place near ancient Troy; it is a settlement near the ruins of that oldest of cities and the one most celebrated by the poets. The entire Homeric epic, a poem which had a very great influence on the ancient world was, as you know, inspired by Troy.

My personal memory concerns the first journey I made to the Near East with some bible scholars. We had visited Palestine, Syria, and Turkey; we had been to Troas and seen the ruins of Troy. There were about thirty people in our party, of various nationalities (Italian, French, German, English, American, etc.) and I still vividly remember the impression which gradually came over each one of us as we listened to the guide and looked at the remains of the walls of Troy.

There was a sort of euphoria amongst us, almost as if we had become children again, and it seemed to us that memories came back to us, that we could glimpse our youth again through the remains of that ancient culture. We saw Homer once more, the people and the great battles which he described. We were, in fact, experiencing an atmosphere which was very familiar to us. This was not surprising as in my day we spent years studying Homer's poems, first in Italian and then in Greek.

So I can imagine that Paul, an educated man familiar with the great poets, finding himself in Troas and visiting those ruins, must also have felt a great sense of joy and continuity with the past: that fascinating epic era which is still virtually unequalled, not only in the history of classic culture but, in general, in all cultures. Naturally the thought arises that Paul, wearied and bored by the monotony of his daily life, would have been reinvigorated, so preparing him for his amazing vision during the night.

> *So we must fully understand the value of study: through geography, history, physics, maths, literature, we study humanity and its richness, we study ourselves. This realisation widens the horizon of our little everyday reality and prepares us for a great revelation.*

What does this mean for us? It means that when we seriously set ourselves the study of the culture, the history and the lives of people, everyday monotony is nourished by something which transcends us – it is *a longing to enter into a cultural, spiritual and mental communion with the whole of humanity* which has preceded us and which accompanies us. So we must fully understand the value of study: through geography, history, physics, maths, literature, *we study humanity and its richness, we study ourselves.* This realisation widens the horizon of our little everyday reality and prepares us for a great revelation.

The new calling

I shall translate verse 9 literally:

> "During the night a vision came to Paul: a Macedonian standing there appealing to him and saying, 'Come across to Macedonia and help us.' "

What changed Paul's life in that moment? The sense of a *new calling*. Paul had been living through monotonous days, he had even been obliged to interrupt his mission, of which he could be justifiably proud, and here was a "Macedonian". All the words of this verse have a precise meaning. *Macedonian* stands for a great race, that of Alexander the Great and other brave conquerors. A Macedonian stood for pride in power and in culture; "standing", one in the fullness of his powers stood there.

And this man was pleading with Paul, he was pleading with him, at that very moment when Paul did not know what to do, did not understand the reason behind such adversity, and felt he was useless. And yet that Macedonian needed him! He was asking him to act, to get ready to set off, and to help him.

"Help us", or literally "Help we" – *boétheson emìn*. You will remember that we have already come across this plea: it was the father of the epileptic boy who said to Jesus: "Help us". Now the same words were directed at Paul and so the apostle felt that he had in front of him someone who was entreating him as if he were Jesus. Note that it does not say: "Help me", but "Help us". The supplicator is therefore the people, a civilisation, a part of humanity. I imagine that Paul unexpectedly understood the secret meaning of the monotony, stress, frustration, the reason why he should persevere day after day.

> *It was no longer Jesus alone who was calling him but someone who was calling him as if he were Jesus.*

In other words, his eyes were opened. It was no longer Jesus alone who was calling him but someone who was calling him as if he were Jesus. Paul felt himself invested with a great responsibility: here was a people, here was a rich, powerful and proud culture which was nevertheless pleading with the Lord, and Paul was able to do something. The everyday monotony of his days could provide an extraordinary source of help for that culture and for those people.

The call of humanity

To our question *Who, Lord, are you?*, the Lord answered: "I am the Lord who calls you, I am the one who liberates you." For Paul the answer was transformed into "I am humanity calling in the name of the Lord."

At the end of this reflection of ours, I would like to say to you: you are Paul. Your life may be fundamentally serene but it is nevertheless demanding; it is a participation in the human suffering of so many people – those who are ill, those who suffer, families in difficulty, the unemployed. Compared with their lives, yours unfolds peacefully despite its occasional monotony, and you must heed the call of a humanity which has need of the Lord, which needs his word, which has need of the service into which you are growing here.

There is something else I want to say to you. The people to whom you must do good are already out there, and there are a great many of them. From now on you can offer your day for them, you can make yourselves responsible for their progress, feeling a sense of solidarity with their suffering and with their searching. If you live in this way, monotony will seem a beautiful and joyous reality to you because each one of you will be able to say: "Through the grace of God, I have something to offer my brothers and sisters and all those who are asking for my help."

"Grant, Lord, that we may understand the magnitude of our responsibility. Grant that from now onwards we may, by virtue of our wearisome daily journey, help many people we know or do not know, through the Communion of Saints. Grant, Lord, that we may be more practical and energetic, imitating the saints. Grant that we may, occasionally, be willing to suffer more so that we may reach out to those who are in difficulties and who are entrusted to our help and to our sacrifice. Grant, Lord, that we may sacrifice ourselves willingly for others who are needy and who say to us: 'Help us, come to our rescue!'"

The road we have travelled
A summary of our journey so far

Before proposing a final reflection on the question *Who, Lord, are you?*, I should like to summarise, for myself and for you, what we have said so far. It may prove useful to put the answers to the question *Who am I?* in a column on the left hand side of the page, and the answers to the question *Who, Lord, are you?* on the right.

In the introduction we started off by suggesting a method of *lectio divina*, in five stages:

1. Re-reading and underlining;
2. Looking for Biblical parallels;
3. Asking, or making of intercession;
4. Offering oneself, or praying prayers of praise;
5. Planning: identifying and developing the subjects you think important.

This is a method which can be used for reading the Gospels and the Bible in general, now and in the future, and I will therefore add a sixth point which will be of help to you:

6. Revising or reflecting on the ground we have already covered.

We will start to carry out this revision by thinking back to those pages of the Bible upon which we have meditated.

Who am I?	*Who, Lord, are you?*

a) Putting ourselves in the place of the widow of Nain's son, we replied:

• I am someone who can say: Thank you! • who can say: I owe you everything, Lord. • who can say: Lord, you have taken me seriously	• You are someone who has said to me: Live, wake up, walk. I am saying this to <u>you</u>. • You are someone who cares about me. • You are someone who meets me half way and calls me.

b) Our reflection on the epileptic boy enabled us to understand other aspects of the answers:

• I am someone who sometimes has difficulty in expressing myself and who must grow into the fullness of human communication. • I am someone who often has to bring order into my feelings and my moods. • I am someone who could harm myself and give way to the temptation of being depressed.	• You are the one who helps me to talk about myself, to express myself. • You are the one who helps me to be objective about what is equivocal and negative about myself. • You are the one to whom I want to entrust myself. • You are my liberator, the one who frees me by means of the truth.

c) What happened to David when he was called on to fight, suggested the following answers to us:

● I am someone you have chosen among many, even though I am less talented, less able than others. ● I am someone to whom you have given the grace not to draw back.	● You are the one to whom I can say: Lord, I walk in your strength, I neither want to give myself airs, nor do I want to draw back. ● You are the one who allows me to express serious purposes for my life, even though I am still young. ● You are my strength against those who would like to stunt my life. The one who has given and will continue to give me victory against my enemies.

d) David's transgression gave us a fuller explanation of the answer to the first question:

● I am someone who sometimes loses my way as a result of small mistakes and who gradually falls into graver errors. ● I am someone who is too ready to make excuses for myself because I think I am clever and eventually I end up in a trap. ● I am someone to whom the Lord gives the strength to say, at least occasionally: "I have made a mistake", helping me to grow up by doing this.	

e) Finally we reflected on the story of Paul at Troas, realising that for each of us the Lord's call can become the call of humanity.

	● I am He who has need of you. I am a humanity, a culture which is asking for your help, the offer of one day of your time, the patience to accept everyday monotony and stress.

The eighth dialogue
The story of Stephen

Now we reflect on a biblical passage which will help us deepen our understanding of the Lord. This is one of the stories which appeals to me most and I have meditated at length upon it; you will find it in the book of Acts of the Apostles, chapter 7. We are at the end of Stephen's speech, in which he has spoken with courage, defended himself against the accusations, and has said freely what he thinks. How do his accusers react?

"They were infuriated when they heard this, and ground their teeth at him. But Stephen, filled with the Holy Spirit, gazed into heaven and saw the glory of God and Jesus standing at God's right hand. 'Look! I can see heaven thrown open,' he said, 'and the Son of man standing at the right hand of God.' All the members of the council shouted out and stopped their ears with their hands; then they made a concerted rush at him, thrust him out of the city and stoned him. The witnesses put down their clothes at the feet of a young man called Saul. As they were stoning him, Stephen said in invocation, "Lord Jesus, receive my spirit." Then he knelt down and said aloud, "Lord, do not hold this sin against them." And with these words he fell asleep."
Acts 7:54–60

This is one of the most complete stories of the New Testament because in it the figure of the Christian achieves total identification with Jesus. I will limit myself to considering four aspects of it with you:

1. Fear;
2. Looking upwards;
3. the Vision;
4. the Offering.

Fear

We can imagine Stephen surrounded by a great crowd united in their anger against him. He realises he is on his own, that he has no-one on his side and he understands that things are turning out badly. He is experiencing the situation of someone who, having made a courageous stand for Jesus, finds he must face mockery, derision, calumny and bullying.

Anyone who has said to the Lord: "You are my Lord, I will follow you", will sooner or later go through what Stephen is going through, albeit in a less dramatic way. You have probably already experienced this yourselves: having made a certain choice, because of your desire to answer the Lord's call, you sometimes meet with a little coldness from someone, you feel alone, perhaps you are teased, you become the object of a caustic remark, are derided in some way. All this makes us understand that we have made a difficult choice which defines us. During my pastoral visits, I realise that there are young men training for the priesthood who have encountered these problems and they tell me about them: "We said and did such and such, and because of it people steer clear of us at school, they exclude us, they jeer at us." This is undoubtedly a difficult predicament but in it we share the predicament of Jesus and his choices.

While on the one hand opting for the Lord puts us alongside people, in fellowship with people, it also means we are faced with situations which often involve exclusion, opposition, criticism. It is therefore not surprising that we are filled with fear: no-one likes to find themselves alone, among people who do not understand or who are hostile! It is for this very reason that the choice for Christ is a brave choice. If it did not carry with it a risk of being misunderstood, we would never say anything truthful and we would end up by adapting ourselves to the way of the world, saying only what pleases other people.

> *Stephen is therefore the model of someone who sometimes has to face hostility and who can be filled by fear.*

Naturally, it can happen, and in fact often does happen, that an act of courage meets with people's approval. Then we hear them say: "At last! Here's someone who can say something different, here is someone who takes life seriously!" Stephen is therefore the model of someone who sometimes has to face hostility and who can be filled by fear.

Looking upwards

Let us try to ask him: "What did you do, Stephen, at that moment? First of all you could have been frightened when you realised that your enemies were in deadly earnest, they were not just saying things, they were not just uttering judgements. You realised that something irrevocable was about to happen. Of course, you could have said you were sorry that you had talked that way and had raised your voice, you could have said that you hadn't explained yourself properly. Or you could even have given in, admitting that your enemies were right because they were stronger than you. However, you would have none of this." The Bible says: "...Stephen, filled with the Holy Spirit, gazed into heaven and saw the glory of God..." (v. 55). Here we read the true discovery of the presence of Jesus within us.

> *When we agree to enter into*
> *difficult situations, the Lord allows*
> *us to experience a strength and a*
> *joy we have never known before:*
> *we realise then that we are in the*
> *truth of the Lord, that we have*
> *made the right choice.*

Who, Lord, are you? You are the one who gives us strength in difficult moments. We have already said this when we talked about Jacob who felt the divine strength during his time of trial. When we agree to enter into difficult situations, the Lord allows us to experience a strength and a joy we have never known before: we realise then that we are in the truth of the Lord, that we have made the right choice.

Stephen, inspired by the Holy Spirit, feels a sense of release, tranquillity, an enthusiasm which do not come from himself. On his own, Stephen could be intimidated, afraid, uncertain; at that moment, however, once he is committed to his act of courage, he experiences the Holy Spirit working in him. Is it not, perhaps, true that Jesus promised his disciples this? 'But when you are handed over, do not worry about how to speak or what to say; what you are to say will be given to you when the time comes, because it is not you who will be speaking; the Spirit of your Father will be speaking in you.' 'When they take you before synagogues, and magistrates and authorities, do not worry about how to defend yourselves or what to say, because when the time comes, the Holy Spirit will teach you what you should say.' (Matthew 10:19–20; Luke 12:11–12)

> *The Holy Spirit gives him the*
> *courage to look upwards, to say:*
> *"Lord, my strength comes from*
> *you," and to see the glory of God.*

This is the ability to *look upwards*. Instead of looking around him, of sizing up the strength of the enemy, of thinking about running away, or hiding, or defending himself, Stephen looks towards his source of strength. The Holy

104

Spirit gives him the courage to look upwards, to say: "Lord, my strength comes from you," and to see the glory of God. This is how Stephen realises that the significance of what is happening to him is not to be found in the accusations and hostility of the people but in the power of God in whose hands is the history of the world.

> *To look upwards is to have the courage which comes from this choice, and the Lord gives us this courage so that we may know more clearly who he is for us.*

In this way we can understand the courage of the martyrs: the martyrs of the past and the martyrs of today, still living, of all ages and social and cultural backgrounds. I have personally been able to meet some of them: when they found themselves attacked and tortured for witnessing to Christ, in that very moment they experienced a totally new clarity and strength. It is as if suddenly our eyes are opened and we see that Jesus is on our side, that we are with him, that God is in charge of history. When others are hostile to us, we feel absolutely certain that we are on the side of God, on the side of truth.

To look upwards is to have the courage which comes from this choice, and the Lord gives us this courage so that we may know more clearly who he is for us.

The Vision

What does Stephen see when he looks upwards?
"The glory of God, and Jesus standing at God's right hand. 'Look! I can see heaven thrown open,' he said 'and the Son of man standing at the right hand of God.'" If we read the Bible carefully, we find other times when Jesus is called the Son of man.

The reason for this is that *Jesus* denotes *the person of Jesus*: the Son of God, who was historically born in Bethlehem, lived in Nazareth, preached in Galilee, and who died and rose again. The description of him as the *Son of man*, however, denotes *Jesus* as *head of the Church*, of all that Church which he carries with him to the fullness of eternal life. *Stephen therefore sees Jesus both as a person and as head of the Church, Lord of the whole of human history.* "Here am I," thinks Stephen, "confronted by a group of people who are shouting, yelling, accusing me. Yet I see and I know that the whole of human history is directed by this Jesus who is the Lord of all and leads and draws them to himself."

> *We comprehend that the sacrifice, offering, and suffering of our lives, lived for Jesus, are all worthwhile. He is the Son of God, he is my liberator, my saviour, the one who has guided me to personal fulfilment.*

It is a vision which widens our horizon to encompass the whole universe and the whole of history. Through this experience we are given the grace to rise above our limited everyday surroundings and are be able to embrace the universality of history. He is the one who has helped me to express myself, who has saved me from the snares of life, who has fashioned me as a living person and filled me with his gifts. He is the master and Lord of universal history. Following him, I follow the Lord of all reality and, in the fullness of his life and of his own death, I am also personally fulfilled.

This is the all-embracing vision of the Church which Stephen attains through suffering and persecution.

The Offering

The vision is followed by the moment of the *offering* or *oblation*. Stephen exclaims: 'Lord Jesus, receive my spirit,' in other words, "Lord, I am yours. *I offer you my life*. You, Lord, have opened the heavens to me and you have made me see momentous realities which I could never have imagined. You made me part of an awesome plan, which is the plan of God the Father. You have revealed a miraculous path to me. Lord, receive my life, receive myself."

This is the experience to which that young man of 35 bore witness for me, when I met him during a pastoral visit a few days before he died. When he said to me: "How great is the Lord! Yes, Lord, I offer my life to you, I thank you for everything, I praise you and I bless you," it truly seemed as if he saw the heavens open!

And I should like each one of you, in the particular vocation to which the Lord calls you, to be able to pray in this way: "You, Jesus, are the Lord of life and history, Lord of the Church and of humanity. I thank you for having called me to take part, in some way, in your service, in your plan. For this plan, Jesus, I offer myself willingly. Take me, Lord, because this plan is yours."

It does not matter if you are not yet sure which path the Lord has called you to take; what counts is the certainty that he calls us to achieve great things in life *if we entrust ourselves to him.* Each one of us can therefore respond, if we so choose, with absolute certainty.

> *You are the Lord of history, the Son of God, who will never abandon me; you are the one who has called me and welcomes me, sustains me and consoles me, who gives me strength in solitude and in persecution, and who saves me.*

"Lord, I offer you my life." Every Christian should say this, every person who has been baptised. The rest will follow. *Who am I?* Someone who can declare: "Lord, take my life, it is yours, make of me what you will. I love you, Lord, with all my heart and my life because you have loved me with your life and with your death." *Who, Lord, are you?* You are the Lord of history, the Son of

God, who will never abandon me; you are the one who has called me and welcomes me, sustains me and consoles me, who gives me strength in solitude and in persecution, and who saves me.

This is the clarity to which we are called and I ask it for all of you, in the hope that you will ask it for me. We must do this every day, especially in times of difficulty and times of trial.

Jesus himself wanted to teach us the prayer which asks for the certain knowledge of the kingdom, for strength in temptation, and deliverance from evil. Now we are going to recite it slowly together, thinking about how Stephen might have recited it during the last moments of his life:

> *Our Father who art in heaven,*
> *hallowed by thy name.*
> *Thy kingdom come.*
> *Thy will be done on earth as it is in heaven.*
> *Give us this day our daily bread.*
> *And forgive us our trespasses,*
> *As we forgive those who trespass against us.*
> *And lead us not into temptation,*
> *But deliver us from evil.*

The ninth dialogue
Contemplation of the cross

From the Gospel according to John:

"Near the cross of Jesus stood his mother and his mother's sister, Mary the wife of Clopas, and Mary of Magdala. Seeing his mother, and the disciple whom he loved standing near her, Jesus said to his mother, 'Woman, this is your son.' Then to the disciple he said, 'this is your mother.' And from that hour the disciple took her into his home.

After this, Jesus knew that everything had now been completed and, so that the scripture should be completely fulfilled, he said: 'I am thirsty'. A jar full of sour wine stood there; so, putting a sponge soaked in the wine on a hyssop stick, they held it up to his mouth. After Jesus had taken the wine he said, 'It is fulfilled'; and bowing his head he gave up his spirit.

It was the Day of Preparation, and to avoid the bodies' remaining on the cross during the Sabbath – since that Sabbath was a day of special solemnity – the Jews asked Pilate to have the legs broken and the bodies taken away. Consequently the soldiers came and broke the legs of the first man who had been crucified with him and then of the other. When they came to Jesus, they saw he was already dead, and so instead of breaking his legs one of the soldiers pierced his side with a lance; and immediately there came out blood and water. This is the evidence of one who saw it – true evidence, and he knows that what he says is true –and he gives it so that you may

believe as well. Because all this happened to fulfil the words of scripture: 'Not one bone of his will be broken';
And again, in another place scripture says:
'They will look to the one whom they have pierced'."
John 19:25–37

Whilst praying we have meditated on the Stations of the Cross, the last journey of Jesus which was to end on Calvary. I should like to express two thoughts which may be of help to you in your private meditation.

> *While I am there I always feel that I am at the centre of the world, and I understand that the world appeared in all its truth only when it was surveyed from the cross, through the eyes of Jesus.*

The light which comes from the cross

For me Jerusalem is the most beautiful and the most precious place in the world. In Jerusalem is the Calvary Chapel, in the Church of the Holy Sepulchre. Some of you will have already been there, others will certainly go there, sooner or later. Climbing up a flight of steps, you come to a chapel where there is a small altar reserved for the Greek monks and here you can pause for prayer. Under the altar there is a hole which is said to mark the place where the wooden upright of the cross of Jesus was driven into the ground. Behind it, a large Byzantine panel shows Jesus on the cross, Our Lady, the Apostle John and Mary Magdalene.

I have spent so many hours of my life in this little chapel and I never tire of lingering there, spending a long time in silent prayer without managing to say anything special. While I am there I always feel that I am at the centre of the world, and I understand that the world appeared in all its truth only when it was surveyed from the cross, through the eyes of Jesus.

Today I still continue with this fundamental prayer which is the contemplation of the cross as the meaning of, and key to, all human history. There is no-one, no human condition which cannot be related to this contemplative listening to the message of the cross. I therefore ask Jesus for this grace for each of you: that you should be able to contemplate more and more the light which streams from his cross, to connect every reality of your lives and every reality of history to the cross.

The love of Christ crucified

The second thought was suggested to me by the Gospel passage to which we have just listened. Reflecting on it, I understood that John also ascribed a fundamental importance to the cross.

If, moreover, we read the prologue of the fourth Gospel ("In the beginning was the Word…The Word became flesh, he lived among us; and we saw his glory"), we realise that from the very beginning John was writing whilst thinking of and looking at the cross. His entire Gospel can be re-read as a deepening of this contemplation. This explains the stress he places on the last part of his description of Jesus' death: "This is the evidence of one who saw it – true evidence, and he knows that what he says is true – and he gives it so that you may believe as well" (19:35).

John makes this affirmation because he believes that the contemplation of the cross is extremely important. In the symbols of water and blood – which are signs of death and of life – he sees the culmination of the revelation of a merciful and faithful God who, by love, gives life to humanity.

From the symbolic vision of the water and the blood, John unexpectedly understands all over again *who God is for humanity: God is the one who passionately loves us. And we, who are we? We are the ones who were regarded and loved by Jesus from the cross.* Our existence is given new life by that water and by that blood which are, for us, Baptism and the Eucharist. Baptism, whose grace grows and develops with our faith, to our Confirmation, and then continues to the Sacraments of Christian responsibility: Marriage or Holy Orders. The Eucharist is our daily nourishment and is to be maintained through meditation on the word of God.

All this is present in the contemplation of the cross.

> *"O Mary, mother of Jesus, you who stood by the cross and contemplated its mystery of pain and love, grant that we may willingly be with you and willingly prolong our stay in this mystical Jerusalem, meditating on the mystery which is the key to our entire life and to human history."*

A continuing answer

We have come to the last meeting of our retreat and I want to thank you for having shared with me in the faith; I have listened with great interest and been enriched and filled with great happiness. I very much admired your ability to express yourselves, perhaps because at your age I was not able to do this so effectively.

When we started our meditations I was wondering whether I would be able to make myself understood by you young people. I was afraid that I might not manage to express the truth which the Lord wanted to tell you through me. Now I realise that it is not really important whether I have succeeded or fallen short: what counts is that you kept your attention fixed upon our chosen path. From your letters and from individual meetings with you, I have, in fact, been able to sense your great willingness to listen and your deep longing to know the Lord. So I am grateful to you for having put me at my ease and for having allowed yourselves to be guided by the Holy Spirit.

Our two questions revisited

Who am I?

One of the themes which emerged from your reflections is that of education. The Gospel story of the epileptic boy who was unable to express himself, to communicate, suggested this theme to us. To educate oneself means to learn how to express the exceptional values we have within ourselves. This ability is the source of an immense joy, it is a cause for such rejoicing that anything else of value – including gold and silver! – is of secondary importance.

> *Only when we fail to learn to express ourselves and to communicate the values which we have inside ourselves do we then turn to the pursuit of gold. Money becomes the measure of our worth, of our importance, of whether we are someone in the eyes of the world.*

Your presence, however, is proof of God's ability to communicate with people, and that of people to communicate with each other. One of you asked me: "What will the truths we have been thinking about here mean to us when we are confronted by the uncaring everyday world again?" I believe that the secret lies in never separating the questions which we have asked ourselves: "Who am I? Who are you?"

Every person, at least implicitly, answers the first question sooner or later. Society today teaches that a person is alive insofar as they have an idea of themselves. If this idea is destroyed, various forms of psychosis arise which can even lead to suicide.

It is not enough, however, to answer the first question, because I only understand who I really am when I place myself in front of a "you", when I enter into a dialogue with the Lord. It is this which makes a person different, new and true; this is the fundamental point.

You are the same as other young people: like them, you eat, drink, study, play, work, and pray. What makes you different from others and makes you free is the fact that you have chosen to answer the second question: "Who are you for me, Lord?" Your decision is a momentous act, which can change history. If you carry on day after day wanting to answer in the same way, you will certainly be able to grow into the fullness of your humanity, into the fullness of joy. If you enter into a dialogue with the Lord every day, allow yourselves to be questioned and called by him, the work done during our reflections and prayers during this time spent on retreat can only strengthen your awareness that humankind can only understand itself in relation to that "you" which is the Lord.

Who are You?

How does the Lord reveal himself to us? First and foremost in his word. *You are the word of God*. A real understanding of the word of God equates to the understanding of who I am, understanding why I am sometimes happy and why, at other times, I suffer or am troubled. The word is a "you" which explains me and I must learn to read it in the Bible by praying: "Lord, you made me and this word is the same as that which created me in the beginning." I start off by listening in silence; I reflect; I answer; I ask. Prayer must always be an answer to the "you", to the word.

You are also the Church. I understand myself by trusting Jesus who is in the Church, who becomes the Church. It is therefore necessary to listen and follow what the Church – the Pope, Bishops, Superiors, my spiritual director – advise me to do.

But I must also learn to see *the Lord who talks to me and reveals his greatness to me in every creature and in all God's works*. The whole of life must join in the dialogue with Jesus, which comes from prayer, from listening to the Word, from relationships with the Church, from cultural considerations, from care for others, and from listening to people in general.

If the Lord is the one who saves me and endows me with truth, if I have accepted that the Lord should be my "you" for my life, this redeems every other value. Situations will alter, external or internal cultural conditions will change; tomorrow we will be able to do things which we cannot do today. However, *the fundamental meaning of existence is to have understood who the Lord is for me*, in relation to myself. God's word remains even when everything changes or passes, God's word is an indestructible rock. At the moment when Peter said to Jesus: "You are the Christ, the Son of the living God," he also discovered himself and Jesus reinforced this when he replied: "I say to you: *you are* Peter." When we really understand this fundamental dialogue, we understand so many things and we will be able to bear witness to that "you" which we have learnt to know and which has given us an awareness of our being.

When I think of you all, I have faith that the Lord will continue to inspire faithful witnesses from within the Church, full of strength, enthusiasm and constancy. He who has wrought marvels in David, in Mary, and in the Apostles, will ensure that many, many more saints emerge from the humility and simplicity of daily life.

> *"O Mary, you who were able to make your life a continuous and uninterrupted dialogue with the Lord, grant that we may continue to know him as the truth of our existence, and to be able to express this every day with joy and serenity."*